£5

Architecture of the World

SCHOOL OF ART
STROUD
PLEASE DO NOT REMOVE

LANSDOWN

Andreas Volwahsen
Henri Stierlin (Ed.)

India

Photos: Andreas Volwahsen
Preface: Walter Henn

Benedikt Taschen

Editor of Series Henri Stierlin
Plans Andreas Volwahsen and Gerd Mader

Editions Office du Livre, Lausanne
Printed in Germany
ISBN 3-8228-9301-3

Contents

The Significance of the Grid

Foreword

By Walter Henn, Architect

It is difficult for a European to find the right approach to Indian architecture. Even parallels with modern architecture soon prove to be wholly misleading, and one seeks familiar guidelines from European buildings, or at least looks for points of comparison, only to be disappointed that no such aids to orientation are immediately recognizable. Even simple comparison of elements of style is of no help to the student who comes from an alien background.

In India, just as one's view is obscured by the luxuriant vegetation of the jungle, so in architecture one is overwhelmed by the immense wealth of forms, of decorative ornament and sculpture. But this makes it all the more delightful to penetrate through these externals and to inquire what canons or laws governed the work of the ancient Indian architects. Medieval Indian architecture in particular, with its numerous Hindu temples, invites such an inquiry.

The studies carried out for this book, and now made accessible to the general public, lead to astonishing conclusions. One encounters some quite simple regular forms, such as the square and the equilateral triangle. Furthermore, the regular arrangement of identical squares produces a very strict grid plan, which serves as a basis for almost all Hindu temples. The square and the equilateral triangle, on account of their symmetrical structure, are always related to the circle as well.

Once one has grasped the geometric principles underlying Indian architecture, one is bound to draw comparisons with corresponding epochs of European architecture. Parallels with modern architecture are also manifest. Modern architecture is sometimes reproached for being poorer than that of earlier eras, since most buildings today are constructed on the basis of a grid plan. Yet by contrast Indian architecture does not seem to have suffered any kind of limitation upon its wealth of forms by using such grids, even figures so rigid and unyielding as squares. Is it possible that this profusion was only able to develop 'because' it was based upon a grid?

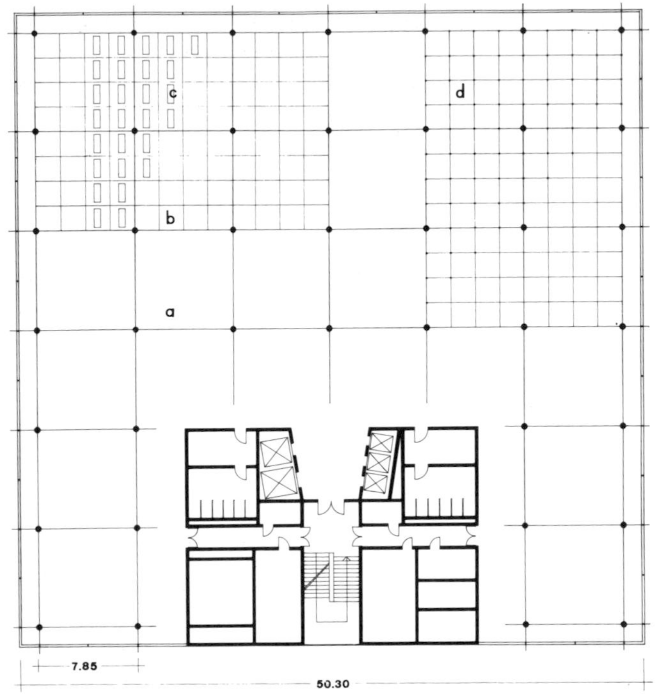

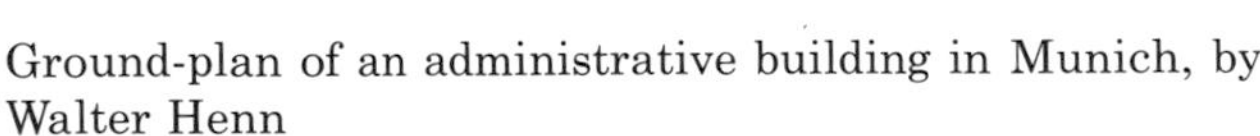

Ground-plan of an administrative building in Munich, by Walter Henn
a) grid plan of supporting framework c) grid plan of ceilings
b) grid plan of floor installations d) grid plan of lighting

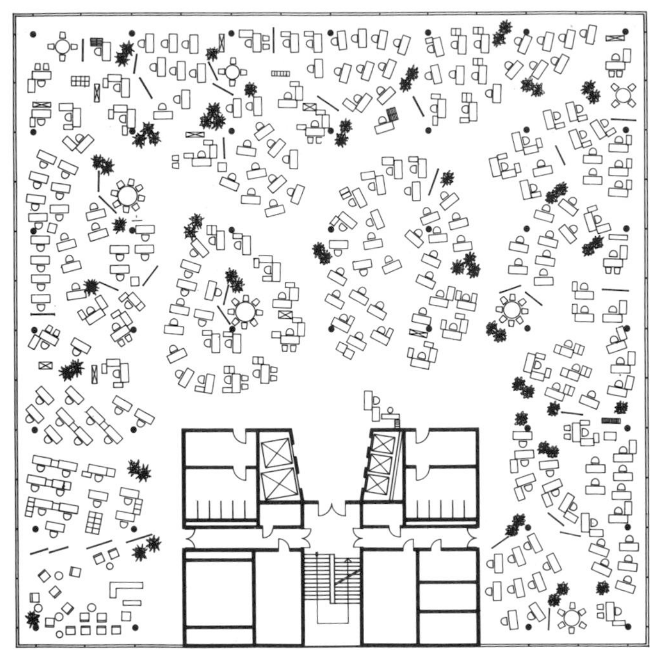

Ground-plan of the same area with 'open-plan' arrangement of furniture

In Indian architecture the use of the square as the basic unit and of the triangle as the principle governing the layout was chiefly a matter of religious significance. Each square was thought to be the abode of a deity, and the location of the square within the ground-plan accorded with the importance attached to that deity. The square in the centre of each building was the seat of Brahman. The Indian architect was solely concerned with the religious significance of the grid he used. Thus a Hindu temple can be interpreted as a model of the cosmos serving purposes of religious worship.

When we employ a grid in a modern functional building, we do so mainly from economic considerations (or so at least it seems from a superficial point of view). We try to use identical architectural elements which can be mass-produced. We are also prepared to modify the grids upon which our buildings are based whenever this seems expedient or economically worthwhile.

The Indian architect could not modify his basic geometric figures, because these were of religious origin. Therefore he kept to the ancient forms and repeated them, in completely different materials, as the centuries passed. It follows that Indian architects were not familiar with the notion of building in such a way as to do justice to the qualities of the material; instead the canonization of forms was uppermost in their work. Such concepts as thrust, support and arch, taken from European architecture, do not apply in a consideration of Indian architecture. Indeed, even the term façade carries a different connotation.

Since for the Indian priest-architect the square was the mystical, absolute, basic form, which did not permit any variation in the course of construction, it could all the more easily be embellished with abundant decoration, and could even be virtually obscured from view. This decoration, especially the sculpture, was iconographic in character.

Now, in our modern buildings a development is taking place which likewise is obscuring the grid. In the 'open-plan' method of designing a large modern office it is hardly possible to identify the underlying grid plan. This freedom to exploit an area organizationally is, however, only possible because several grids have been harmonized with each other in a wholly consistent manner, starting with the foundations, going on to the installations in the floors, and ending with the partitioning of the low ceilings and

Working model of large office, by Walter Henn, showing the 'open-plan' arrangement of the personnel according to working groups

Ground-plan of a Hindu temple built on a square grid

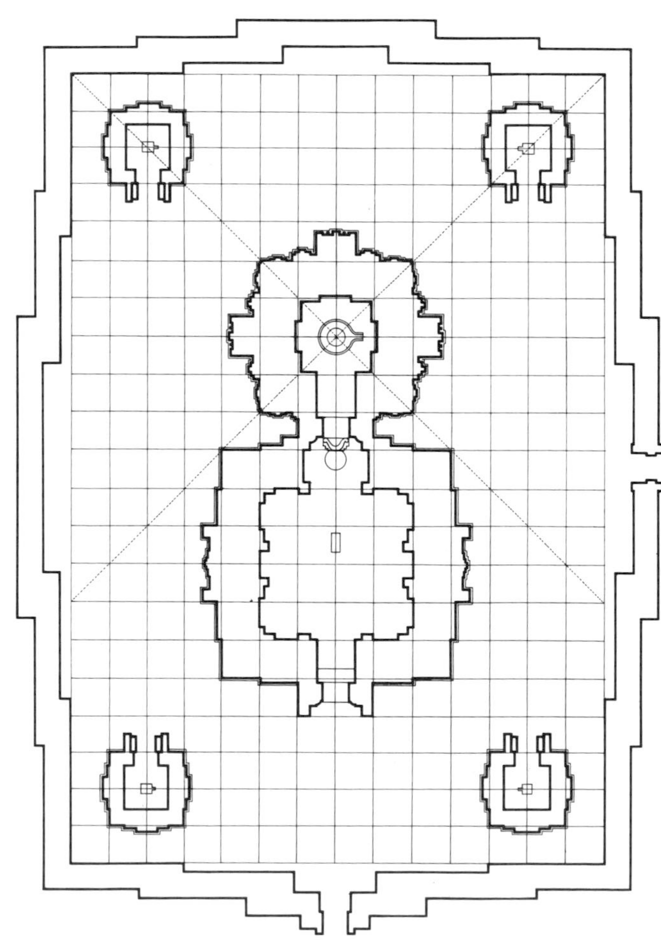

the arrangement of the lighting. We would probably be unable to solve the problems of modern building in a rational way without the basic geometric patterns which the grid plan provides. For it is not only the obvious technical and economic considerations, or simple principles of regularity, which make the modern architect design his buildings on the basis of a grid. In the long run he does so because he has the urge to create – to create something consciously instead of letting it grow organically – which presupposes a commitment to a geometric order. It depends upon the intensity of the challenge presented by each specific architectural problem whether one can develop an independent and convincing form on the basis of a grid, or whether this grid must become the Procrustes' bed of modern architecture.

However strange Indian architecture may seem to us, and as little as we may suspect at first glance that it bears any relation to modern architecture, it is all the more stimulating to trace the effect which the underlying geometric grid has upon Indian buildings, an effect that is still of importance for us today. Different motivations have led to totally different kinds of building. The only possible inference one can draw from this is that a grid as such is devoid of any architectonic value. It is only the meaningful content with which it is invested by the architect that determines its effect.

1. Introduction: The Historical and Religious Foundations

India owes the unusual continuity of her cultural development primarily to her geographical isolation. Since the earliest times this geographical situation has given the inhabitants a false sense of security. Once invaders had penetrated into the country, they found it easy to conquer.

Thus in the second millennium B.C. a pastoral equestrian people from the plateaux of Central Asia overran one town after another on the Indus plain, which already possessed a very highly developed culture but was militarily weak. These conquerors were called Aryans. For the next two thousand years they set the tone of intellectual, and in particular of social, life in India. The antagonism between aliens and natives gave rise to a system of castes and sub-castes which became ever more complex as time went on. The Aryans' religious beliefs, which were confined to the worship of certain natural phenomena, came up against a world inhabited by innumerable spirits and demons. The results of this encounter can be seen even today, in the existence of a plethora of concepts and cults so diverse that it is difficult to describe them adequately. These contrasts led to the creation of inexhaustible treasure in the fields of philosophy and art. On the other hand, such variety was an obstacle to unity against the threat of attack by foreign enemies. From the tenth century A.D. onwards Mohammedan peoples, who, like their predecessors, entered the country from the north-west, were able to raid and seize north India without great difficulty. The invaders, like the Aryans, destroyed a great deal of the culture they found in India. After the indigenous Dravidian population of the Indus plain had been subjugated by the Aryans the Indus valley civilization was wiped out. Similarly, after the Muslim conquest of north India, there could be no further independent development of Hindu architecture. For this reason we shall here be concerned with a particular period in the history of Indian architecture.

Three periods may be distinguished in the history of Indian architecture:

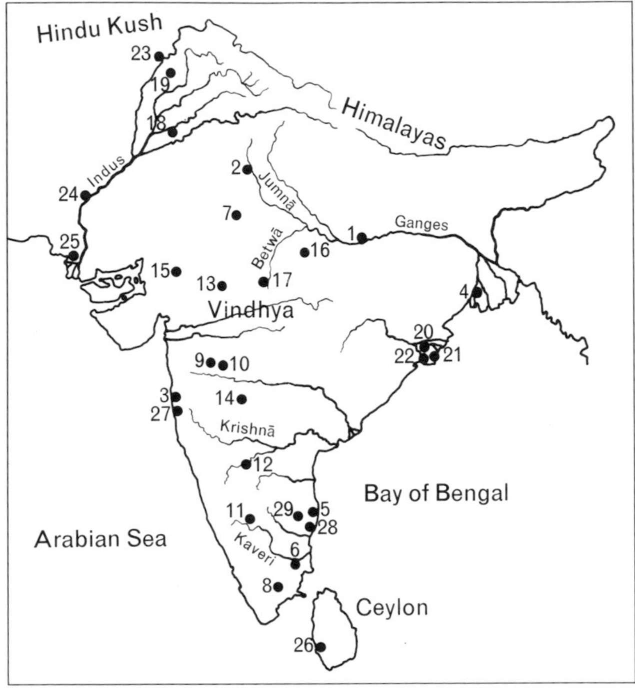

Map of India

1 Kashi (Benares)	11 Somnāthpur	21 Konārak
2 Delhi	12 Vijayanagar	22 Caurasi
3 Bombay	13 Ujjain	23 Takht-i-Bāha
4 Calcutta	14 Chezarla	24 Mohenjo-daro
5 Madras	15 Ābū	25 Karachi
6 Tanjore	16 Khajurāho	26 Colombo
7 Jaipur	17 Sāñchī	27 Kārlī
8 Madurai	18 Harappā	28 Mahaballipuram
9 Elūrā	19 Taxila	29 Kanchipuram
10 Ajantā	20 Bhuvaneshvar	

1. The architecture of the Indus valley civilization, from about 2500 B.C. to the Aryan invasion about 1500 B.C.;
2. Hindu architecture, from the Aryan invasion to the gradual conquest of India by the Mohammedans, i.e. to the thirteenth century A.D.;
3. Islamic architecture, from the tenth to the eighteenth centuries A.D., when the Muslim rulers were succeeded by a British administration. In this book we shall deal with the second of these three periods, since it alone reflects the essential features of the Hindu genius. But as this period is itself the product of a long process of historical evolution, we shall begin with a brief sketch of the preceding urban civilization of the Indus valley.

Indus valley civilization

The first evidence of a pre-Aryan civilization was brought to light by Sir John Marshall, who excavated the remains of Mohenjo-daro and Harappā, two cities on the Indus plain. Both were constructed on a rectangular plan and it was a remarkable fact that, although they were more than 600 kilometres apart, the principles of their layout were identical. Subsequent excavations in north-east India have brought to light remains of several smaller cities which must have belonged to the same civilization. These discoveries caused a complete revision of the accepted view of early Indian history, which had in any case been uncertain for the period prior to the seventh century B.C.

Even so, little is known about the origins of the Indus valley civilization, because at Mohenjo-daro the high level of ground-water on the site prevented archaeologists from digging down through the earliest, lowest strata and reaching the virgin soil beneath. The finds made in the upper strata indicate that, unlike the metropolises of the contemporary civilization of Mesopotamia, the city did not begin as a small settlement and grow slowly along the bank of a river, but was built as an integral unit: it is indeed the earliest example of what may be called town planning. The main streets, which formed an almost perfect rectangle, divided it into separate residential areas; these in turn were divided by side streets, also set at right angles; and finally the individual residential areas were separated by footpaths. The houses had no windows facing the street, but instead the living and sleeping quarters were built around an inner court, as is still the custom today over much of the east. The supporting parts of the houses were exclusively of brick. Even some large buildings, identified as nobles' palaces, were executed in brick of this kind, bereft of any decoration. The houses were of the same height throughout. Lacking here is the conspicuous palace so characteristic of early cities in the Near East, but both at Mohenjo-daro and at Harappā the residential quarter is dominated by an artificial mound of brick which, in contrast to the residential area itself, is strongly fortified. This citadel, interestingly enough, does not contain the splendid palace of an absolute oriental ruler but – in Mohenjo-daro, for example – a vast bathing establishment, granaries and other communal installations. The city possessed a complex irrigation and drainage system, so perfect that its equal is to be found only in Rome.

Attemps have frequently been made to link the cities of the Indus valley with the urban civilization of Sumer, and even to classify them as non-Indian offshoots of the latter. The fact that seals from the Indus valley have been found in Mesopotamia, and that the worship of fertility symbols is common to both civilizations, supports such hypotheses. In the Indus valley there is a marked difference between the urban and the rural archaeological discoveries, which has led to the conjecture that in prehistoric times an advanced civilization was superimposed upon the

Town plan of Mohenjo-daro (c. 2000 B.C.)

simpler culture of an indigenous people who dwelt in villages. The urban inhabitants already seem to have been familiar with bronze tools, for example, whereas the villagers worked entirely with stone axes. However, in considering the urban social structure, as far as it can be reconstructed from the architectural remains in the cities, it seems unlikely that any connection (other than normal fruitful contacts) existed between the Land of the Five Rivers (the Punjab) and the Land of the Two Rivers (Mesopotamia). Society in Mesopotamia was oriented towards an absolute ruler, whereas at Mohenjo-daro and Harappā we find a broad stratum of prosperous city-dwellers, who were clearly not ruled by a tyrannical despot but by priest-princes whose authority was rooted in laws and religious precepts.

We shall only be able to identify the actual rulers of this vast empire centred upon Mohenjo-daro and Harappā when we have succeeded in deciphering the script used by the peoples of the Indus valley.

The Aryan invasion

Harappā and Mohenjo-daro were destroyed by flood or fire on several occasions during their thousand-year history. Each time the cities were rebuilt upon the walls that remained, without the slightest architectural changes being made. The archaeologist finds that each successive stratum looks much the same. In the uppermost layer there is evidence of the final destruction. Skeletons lying in unnatural postures suggest that the Indus valley civilization was forcibly brought to an end by Aryan tribesmen, who first raided the area with increasing frequency and then pressed forward relentlessly to the east and south.

The light-skinned Aryans, a relatively primitive nomadic people, did not know what to do with the cities they found in the Indus plain. The dark-skinned inhabitants were enslaved and came to form the lowest rank in the system of castes that was now gradually established. This explanation of the origins of the caste system is corroborated by the fact that the Sanskrit word for caste means simply 'colour', and also by the fact that the Aryans supreme god, Indra, is honoured in sacred tradition as 'the destroyer of cities', which indicates that the Aryans knew of cities and that they found them uncongenial.

In the course of a few centuries this savage nomadic people became settled agriculturalists, and gradually the villages of their tribal chiefs developed into towns, the centres of small principalities and republics. The ancestors of these new city-builders had completely destroyed the urban civilization of the Indus valley, and their otherwise very detailed legends contain scarcely any mention of them. They must have seemed alien and useless to a nomadic race. For this reason the transformation of their simple village culture into an urban civilization of far greater complexity took place without any connection with, and even without any recollection of, the skilful town planning of their predecessors.

The Vedas and Upanishads

It was the fertility of the hot and humid lowlands that lured the Aryans to the Indus plain from the plateaux and mountains of Central Asia. Surrounded by the luxuriant but deadly jungle, they too experienced the fascination of the world of demons and magic in which their dark-skinned subjects had believed for so long. The ancient Aryan belief in 'devas', 'the bright ones', was superseded by fear of the spirits of the impenetrable primeval forest, with its constant growth and decay. In their society, which had originally been moulded by the spirit of its dominant warrior caste, greater influence came to be wielded by tribal priests, or Brahmins, who could afford protection to the villagers from the phantoms of the jungle. Around 1000 B.C. the 'Vedas', a collection of sacred hymns and invocations to Aryan deities which had been handed down orally and had virtually ceased to be comprehensible, were provided with detailed commentaries, the 'Brahmānas'. The Vedic sacrificial act, which was designed to propitiate the wind god, the sun god, or the god of thunder and lightning, evolved into a complex and absolutely fixed ritual.

An increasing number of Dravidian deities were brought into the Vedic pantheon. Although the Vedic gods had been visualized as rather human creatures, the Aryans never made any images of them, whereas the villages of their Dravidian slaves teemed with idols and fertility symbols of great variety. From this fusion of two religions Hinduism developed in its classical form, which it still possesses today. Around 800 B.C. the first philosophical treatises, the 'Upanishads', were composed as a supplement to the Vedic hymns. The personified god, whether of Dravidian or Aryan origin, receded into the background. The seers no longer preached the power of the gods and the need to win their favour by sacrifice and worship; they endeavoured rather to understand the law governing the cosmos and to look upon all existence and activity as causally related.

The only reality they recognized was Brahman, 'the self-luminous, omnipresent, uncreated, eternal Self, the ultimate cause of the universe, the power behind all tangible forces, the consciousness which animates all conscious beings'. This is regarded in its transcendental manifestation as the so-called 'uncreated' or 'unformed' Brahman. It cannot be comprehended by reasoning and is thus most readily described by circumlocutory paradoxes, such as the following: 'This Brahman, devoid of any duality, although not moving is faster than thought, although resting travels far, although reclining goes everywhere.'

As purest Being, standing above all causal relationships of space and time, the 'unformed' Brahman is the negation of all attributes. According to the 'Upanishads', whoever perceives it while sunk in meditation is promised union with this purest Being, redemption from the cycle of birth, death and re-birth, and entry into Brahman.

This concept of Brahman as the supreme principle upon which all things are based does not satisfy the believer's need for a personified god, a merciful lord of the universe. For this reason the Brahman in its phenomenal manifestation may also be regarded as the 'formed' Brahmā, or Ishvara. In this manifestation, on the plane of the phenomenal world, Brahman corresponds to God the Father in Christianity or to Allah in Islam. In considering the attributeless Brahman, free from all limitations of space and time, the idea of the creation of the world was irrelevant; the formed Brahmā, on the other hand, can be venerated as the creator, preserver and destroyer of the cognizable universe – a universe which does not represent ultimate reality. In his functions as creator, preserver and destroyer, the ruler of the world is venerated in the first place as creator, again called Brahmā, secondly as preserver, called Vishnu, and thirdly as destroyer, called Shiva. This Hindu trinity of Brahmā, Vishnu and Shiva does not imply that the monotheistic principle has indirectly been abandoned. All these three gods are to be regarded expressly and solely as manifestations of the one Brahman. The same is true of all other gods in the Hindu pantheon. They can in principle be derived from the fundamental trinity as reincarnations, as manifestations conditioned by their function, or as a female principle inseparable from a male deity; and thus they can also be linked, through the formed Brahmā, to the only reality, the uncreated, unformed Brahman.

Deities in the Hindu religion are only products of the imagination, which exist solely on the plane of the phenomenal world. They are designed to enable the believer to worship those attributes which he deems divine of the Supreme Being, who himself has no attributes yet encompasses all of them. Various sects project these three functions of creation, preservation and destruction upon one of the three deities mentioned. Thus, for example, the Shivaites regard only Shiva, and the Vishnuites only Vishnu, as simultaneously creator, preserver and destroyer.

The created Brahmā, dependent upon phenomena such as space and time, provides the yardstick for Hindu chronology. A Brahmā lives for 100 Brahmā years. Upon his death a cosmic system comes to an end, to develop again with the birth of a new Brahmā. A day of Brahmā, known as a 'kalpa', lasts for 1000 Great Ages of the World, or 'mahā yugas'. One mahā yuga in turn consists of four successive Great Ages of the World: 'krita yuga', 'treta yuga', 'dvapara yuga' and 'kali yuga'. During the krita yuga, which lasts for 4000 divine years, the world is a paradise; men are good and live happily. During the treta yuga, which comprises 3000 divine years, men's happiness is limited by the growth of envy and selfishness. During the 2000 divine years of the dvapara yuga these negative tendencies become more pronounced, until finally the moral degradation of man is brought to an end, after the kali yuga, which lasts only 1000 divine years, by a partial end of the world. Since one divine year is equal to 360 sidereal years, the following reckoning may be made: one mahā yuga comprises 4,320,000 sidereal years; one day of Brahmā comprises 4,320,000,000 sidereal years; Brahmā lives for 311,040,000,000,000 sidereal years. Today we are living in a kali yuga. This universe will end in A.D. 428,898.

The belief in a supreme law, according to which all existence is subject to change, to growth and decay – a law which man can comprehend only by observing the succession of the seasons, and can calculate by observing the stars – led the seers to the doctrine of the re-birth of the soul. To the question: what is the criterion determining entry into a new life? they replied by developing the theory of a causality of retribution.

During the first half of the first millennium B.C. this doctrine spread throughout India, except for certain areas in the south. The social and religious order became fixed in the forms laid down in the sacred texts. Hitherto it had been possible for a man to move from one caste to another, for example by changing his means of livelihood. A Brahmin could become a warrior and thus enter the caste of Kshatriyas, and 'vice versa'; it was even possible for an able descendant of a dark-skinned Dravidian slave to rise to the rank of a Brahmin. But the more the Brahmins sought to isolate themselves from the other castes on account of their possession of occult knowledge, the keener members of the other castes, even the lowest one, became to observe the strict lines of demarcation between them.

Gautama Buddha

In 563 B.C., during this time of questing for a fixed point of certainty in the deceitful external world, Gautama Siddhārtha was born in a small principality at the foot of the Himalayas. On the occasion of his birth it was foretold to his father, the ruling prince, that his son would become famous either as a great seer or as a statesman. His father preferred to have him become a statesman rather than a monk, and surrounded him with all the luxuries of a prosperous court of an Aryan prince. Siddhārtha was above all kept in ignorance of the darker side of earthly life, the knowledge of which was clearly responsible for the unworldliness of the Hindu spiritual leaders. But despite all precautionary measures on four occasions the prince made journeys away from his home, and so he met, successively, a sick man, a frail old man, a funeral procession and finally, on his fourth journey, an ascetic of majestic demeanour, who strode across his path. Shaken by the sight of human suffering, Siddhārtha decided to follow the holy man's example. One night he left the palace by stealth and for six years kept company with a group of five ascetics. He left them when he found that asceticism was not bringing him any closer to his goal, cognition of true reality. Accordingly he renounced a life of self-castigation and, seated beneath a fig-tree (Bodhi tree), plunged himself for a month into meditation. Finally he was granted the enlightenment he strove to attain, and perceived the laws governing all existence.

Before the five ascetics from whom he had parted in disillusionment, he now preached his first sermon on the 'dharma' (law):

'Now this, O monks, is the noble truth of pain: birth is painful, old age is painful, sickness is painful, death is painful. Contact with unpleasant things is painful, not getting what one wants is painful.

Now this, O monks, is the noble truth of the way that leads to the cessation of pain: this is the noble Eightfold Path, namely, right views, right intention, right speech, right action, right livelihood, right effort, right mindfulness, right concentration.'

City gate of Kushinagara, Magadha. After a relief on the Great Stūpa at the South Gate of Sāñchī

The five ascetics became his first disciples. With them the Enlightened One wandered as a preacher through the kingdoms of north India. He attacked the superstition of the Hindus, the sacrifice of animals, and caste society. He called for respect to be shown to all living things, for charity and compassion. In the towns where he preached there sprang up small Buddhist communities and the first monastic groups. At the age of eighty the Buddha died at Kushinagara. His mortal body was cremated with royal honours in accordance with Hindu custom. Over his relics the monks of the new Buddhist order erected so-called 'stūpas', in the form traditional in early India for the tombs of kings and heroes.

The philosophy of these first communities revolved essentially around the theory that all earthly phenomena are distinguished by three criteria. These are: 'anitya', 'inconstant, subject to perpetual change'; 'dhuka', 'painful'; and 'anatma', 'not belonging to anyone, not really existing'. To escape from this false world of pain is the supreme goal. This is not possible by worshipping gods of any kind, since these, too, are unreal. It is only by following the middle way, the Eightfold Path, that the individual can slowly ascend the hierarchy of living creatures and, thanks to the causality of retribution, can become a Bodhisattva, and can finally rise to become a Buddha and so enter 'nirvāna'.

Alexander the Great

While the Aryan princes of north India engaged in endless squabbles over conflicting territorial claims, the first news reached the lands of the Indus plain about the conquests of the Yavana king Iskander – Alexander the Great of Macedon. In 326 B.C., although he was already finding it difficult to supply his troops, he advanced even further eastwards with the object of conquering India. Just as the common assault on Troy had once brought unity among the factious Greek tribes, so the common conquest of India was now to overcome the antagonism between Greeks and Persians. Alexander skilfully exploited the differences among the Indian rulers. Supported by the army of Omphis, king of Gandhāra, he crossed the Hydaspes and the Indus, and reached the borders of the Magadha empire. The conquest of this powerful realm would have brought all India under Macedonian rule. But Alexander's officers were weary of fighting and induced their king to break off the campaign. To safeguard the eastern frontier of his empire Alexander built castles and cities on the Indus, and then returned with his army to Babylon. North India was not hellenized, but in the Buddhist art of Gandhāra traces of Greek influence were to make themselves felt for several centuries.

Alexander's empire collapsed after his death. Chandragupta, the commander of the native troops in Gandhāra, expelled the Greek governor Eudemos and with the aid of his partisans conquered the Magadha empire. For a few years he held sway over the whole of north India. The imperial idea had fallen on fertile soil. Chandragupta's adviser and former teacher, Kautilya, composed the first and only great Indian manual on the art (or rather, cunning) of statesmanship. A secret police force, espionage and deportation were striking features of the new domestic policy which Chandragupta put into effect. On account of his humble origin the king was given the sobriquet 'Maurya'. When he saw that his son, a fervent disciple of Kautilya, was preparing to overthrow him, he renounced the throne while still at the height of his power and left incognito for the Himalayas, where he wandered through the country as a mendicant ascetic.

A similar change of outlook can be observed in the case of Chandragupta's grandson, the Mauryan emperor Ashoka (273–232 B.C.). The first years of his reign were characterized in domestic policy by secret police terror and in foreign policy by the certainty that treaties with neighbouring states would be dishonoured as soon as they had been concluded. After the defeat of the Kalingas on the east coast, the kingdoms of the sub-continent, with the exception of the Dravidian Chola empire at the southern tip, were amalgamated into a Mauryan empire. During the last great battle for Kalinga the 'Machiavellian', or rather 'Kautilyan', king Ashoka was overcome by remorse at the sight of the battlefield strewn with the bodies of the slain. He professed Buddhism and thenceforth abstained from making war–perhaps because he wanted to consolidate his vast empire by making use of this powerful new religion, but maybe also because he was indeed suddenly converted by Buddhist teaching to renounce tyranny and violence, and to respect life instead of indulging in cruel slaughter. The teaching of the Enlightened One now became a state religion. Under the guidance of a mendicant Buddhist monk, Ashoka withdrew from public life for two years, and then returned, as a monk upon the throne, to direct the destinies of his empire for many years. The functions of the secret police were curbed and a body of high-ranking officials set up to make good the injustices that had been committed. The ruler himself wandered through his realm as a mendicant, preaching the new doctrine in even the remotest provincial towns. He had his edicts carved on cliff faces or on memorial pillars erected especially for this purpose. For a pious community of ascetics, the Ājīvikas, he had a number of artificial caves hewn from the granite of the Barābar Hills, so that they might take refuge there during the monsoon season. Over the relics of the Buddha and his disciples he built countless stūpas.

Map of India, showing political situation in the 11th c. A.D. The shaded area indicates the limits of Ashoka's empire

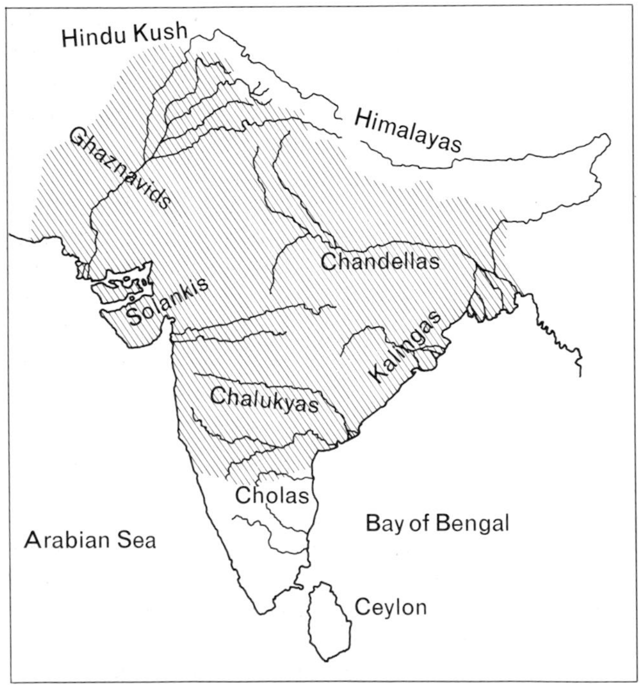

Buddhism alone, however, was unable to keep Ashoka's empire together. Upon his death north India again split into an eastern and western empire. The subjugated Dravidian kings rekindled the old conflict between the dark-skinned natives and their white-skinned Aryan overlords. Soon the sub-continent again presented the familiar picture of feuding petty Hindu kingdoms. A counter-reformation set in, and only the Hindus' deeply ingrained contempt for those of alien belief enabled Buddhism to survive in certain provinces.

In 185 B.C. the last Mauryan emperor was murdered by his commander-in-chief, Pushyamitra. For a century the Shunga dynasty, which he founded, held sway. The Buddhists forfeited all influence at court and the orthodox Shunga kings turned for advice to Brahmin ministers. While the Shungas ruled in the north and the Kalingas in the east, in the south power accrued to the dynasty of the Āndhras. To the south of the Āndhras, the tip of the sub-continent was divided between the Cholas, Keralas and Pandyas.

A Greek colony which lingered on in the Punjab was conquered by invading tribes from Central Asia known as the Shakas. About 100 B.C. another nomadic tribe, under pressure from the advancing Huns, invaded Gandhāra and destroyed the Buddhist empire of the Greek king Hermaios. The new empire of the Kushans, as they were called, extended from the Punjab into Central Asia. Although contemporary sources are sparse for this period, we must say a few words about this dynasty. Once again a change of dynasty brought in its train a change of religion. Kanishka, the only Kushan king about whom relatively detailed accounts have survived, became a Buddhist and summoned a council to Kashmir to clarify interpretations of the doctrine that had long been in dispute. A few years after this council was held a significant change took place in Buddhism. The atheistic doctrine of ethics taught by the Enlightened One became a religion of redemption and salvation. Hinduism, with its vast pantheon of gods, had such a pervasive influence that the Buddha also was elevated to the rank of a god, surrounded by Bodhisattvas (saints who have not yet risen to the rank of a Buddha), honoured and venerated by the Aryan and Dravidian deities who served him.

Ashoka's form of Hīnayāna Buddhism, a dry and intellectual philosophy, had little popular appeal. Under Kanishka's patronage a move was made in the direction of the more easily comprehensible form of Mahāyāna Buddhism. During the Hīnayāna period restraint had been exercised in the figurative portrayal of the Enlightened One, and the Buddha's presence was merely suggested by symbols. From the time of the council onwards countless images of the Buddha as a merciful god abound in monasteries and prayer-halls. The step from Hīnayāna to Mahāyāna recalls the transformation which, in an earlier age, the religion of the Aryan immigrants underwent as a result of the gradual absorption of influences from the older Dravidian beliefs.

From the travel diary kept by a Chinese pilgrim we know that King Kanishka, who was of nomadic origin, did much to promote literature, art and architecture. After the great council he erected a wooden tower, 200 metres high, faced with representations of the Buddha in relief and crowned by a multi-tiered umbrella, the ancient symbol of a ruler. In A.D. 160 Kanishka was strangled. We have no inscription to indicate the dark end that befell the Kushan dynasty.

During the fourth century A.D. the Guptas, former subjects of the Kushans, took over the leadership of the small states of north India. As far as our survey of Indian architecture is concerned, they are of importance because under their rule the first attempts were made to build a temple of stone. The Chinese pilgrim Fa-hsien gives us a picture of the Gupta empire at its height:

'The inhabitants are numerous and happy ...; the king rules without capital or corporal punishment; criminals are sentenced only to a fine which varies according to the gravity of their offence; even in cases of repeated rebellion they merely have their right hand cut off. There are no butchers' shops and no intoxicating beverages are offered for sale ... The king's donations to the Buddhist order are listed on metal plaques, so that they may be handed down from one ruler to another, and none of them may dare to annul any of these gifts. And thus it remains to this day.'

In south India the Cholas, Keralas and Pallavas engaged in internecine conflict for several hundred years. The west coast was under the rule of the Rāshtrakūtas. Of them we know little except that, according to an inscription left by the greatest of their kings, Krishna I (757–783), a sanctuary was built at his command in the hard rock of the mountains of Elūrā. 'Krishna Rāja had a splendid temple built on the mountain of Elapūra. When the gods drove past in their heavenly chariots and saw it, they were very amazed and thought long about the matter. They said to one another: "This temple of Shiva is unique. In no work of art is so much beauty to be found." Even the architect who built it was seized with wonderment, and–in a remark that boded ill for similar efforts in the future–said: "Wonderful! I would not have deemed it possible that I could have created something so beautiful".'

In the south the Keralas built their temples and palaces entirely of wood, so that not a single one of them has survived. From the seventh century onwards, however, the Pallavas made experiments with stone architecture, although only for sacred edifices. At Mahaballipuram (Mamallapuram) they not only carved artificial caves from the rock but also copied in stone various basic types of contemporary wooden building. In the nineteenth century archaeologists unearthed from the sand dunes along the coast of the Gulf of Bengal a monumental stone 'Catalogue of Forms of the Wooden Temple'. At Mahaballipuram, not far from these so-called 'rathas', is the only survivor of the seven temples which the Pallavas erected on the shore, half on land and half in the water, washed on three sides by the sea.

In the tenth century the Cholas brought the whole of south India under their rule. Rāja-rāja the Great founded in his capital city of Tanjore a sanctuary dedicated to Shiva that was larger than any hitherto known. While the Chola empire was its height, in the north-west of the sub-continent Muslim invaders under Mahmud of Ghazni were carrying out the first of their great destructive raids into the prosperous Indus valley. In the eleventh century the Cholas, coming from the south, extended their power into the country of the Kalingas, while the Muslims from the north-west had already reached the borders of the state of Chandella in central India.

In the south the Rāshtrakūtas fell victim to the ambitious family of the Chalukyas, who then attacked the Cholas. New petty kingdoms came into existence, which weakened one another by their perpetual feuding, while in Delhi a former slave, Qutb-ud-din Aibak, took the title of sultan of Delhi. The first Muslim invaders had been content to raid the country in search of booty, but now there was already a strong Muslim state on Indian soil. The sultans, who followed one another in rapid succession, usually dying a violent death, were concerned first of all to strengthen their position at home and then to extend their conquests to central, and ultimately south, India. In the fourteenth century an Islamic ruler held sway even in Madurai. Only the Hindu kingdom around Vijayanagar, founded by the Hoysala family, was able to preserve its independence from the Muslim invaders until the sixteenth century.

Yoga

The Hindu has several ways whereby to attain the supreme goal, union with the Brahman.

'Bhakti yoga', the way of love and devotion, is designated in the 'shāstras', the sacred books, as the way most fitting for those living in the kali yuga. By reciting sacred verses, by singing and by repeating the name of God, the believer falls into the state of mind necessary for the perception of higher things.

In sculpture, bhakti yoga inspired the many thousands of representations of gods and demons found in the temple towns of south India. In Madurai this development can be seen in its most exuberant form.

'Karma yoga' is the way of unselfish conduct. Through worship, i.e. by serving one's fellow creatures, the believer gains insight into the highest form of existence.

'Jñāna yoga' is the way of the intellect, i.e. of philosophical speculation. Thus we may assign to jñāna yoga the 'vedanta' schools, which attempt to conceptualize the inexpressible with the aid of the 'Upanishads'.

'Rāja yoga', the royal way, is quite inappropriate for the kali yuga. One of the first stages along this way, 'hala yoga', the art of controlling one's body, is, however, emulated today in the western world, often in a misunderstood form. Rāja yoga and jñāna yoga lead the believer to the so-called 'nirvikalpa samadi', union with the formless absolute. If this condition lasts for twenty-one days, no return to the phenomenal world is possible.

Plates

Sāñchī

21 Buddhist sanctuary, dating from the 3rd century B.C. The stone casing of the so-called Great Stūpa (in the background) is from the 2nd century A.D. The forms of the Great Stūpa are repeated more simply in Stūpa no. 3 (in the foreground).

22 Stūpa no. 3 from the south-east. The interior consists of rubble masonry, the facing of ashlar masonry. The hemispherical shell, constructed in horizontal courses, is not self-supporting but is sustained by a filling of rubble masonry.

23 In the foreground, the lower stone railing of the Great Stūpa; behind it, the flight of steps leading to the upper circumambulatory path.

24 The hemispherical shell has a smaller diameter than the cylindrical base: hence this upper circumambulatory path.

25 The lower stone railing of the Great Stūpa. Although it is more than 3 metres high, it was modelled exactly upon earlier small wooden fences.

26 The magnificent gates leading to the lower circumambulatory path are covered with reliefs showing scenes from the previous reincarnations of the Buddha. Human beings and animals are skilfully worked into the geometric framework of buildings and other architectural elements.

27 East Gate of the Great Stūpa. The architraves are involuted at the ends. Buddhist monks interpret this motif as an indication that the legends represented could be continued 'ad infinitum'.

Lomas Rishi and Sudāma caves

28 Tympanum on the façade of Lomas Rishi cave (3rd century B.C.). An early stage in the translation of wooden architectural forms into monolithic ones.

29 In the interior of the Sudāma cave stands a monolithic copy of a round house with thatched roof. The Lomas Rishi and Sudāma caves have the same form and measurements, but the former cave was never completed.

Kārlī

30 The subterranean prayer-hall (chaitya-hall) at Kārlī, dating from the 1st century A.D., shows the monolithic combination of circular and rectangular areas to form a basilica.

31 The colonnade dividing the aisle from the nave.

32 The barrel-vaulting.

33 These columns, capitals, carved figures and rafters of the roof – partly hewn directly out of the rock, partly added in wood – make the chamber seem both homogeneous and highly differentiated.

Ajantā

34 The Waghora river cuts a narrow gorge through the plateaux of the western Ghats. The rounded form of the valley seemed to the Buddhist monks particularly well suited for a monastery.

35 Façade of a prayer-hall (chaitya-hall no. 19), dating from the 6th century A.D.

36 In monasteries rounded roofs and windows are repeated for decorative effect.

37 View of the entrance to chaitya-hall no. 19, from an ancillary chamber.

38 Opposite the entrance to monastery no. 2 is the shrine containing an image of the Buddha, instead of a simple monk's cell.

39 Part of the colonnade around the central hall of monastery no. 2.

40 Stūpa in chaitya-hall no. 10, symbolizing the Buddha. Such stūpas were the favourite method of representing the Enlightened One during the Hīnayāna period.

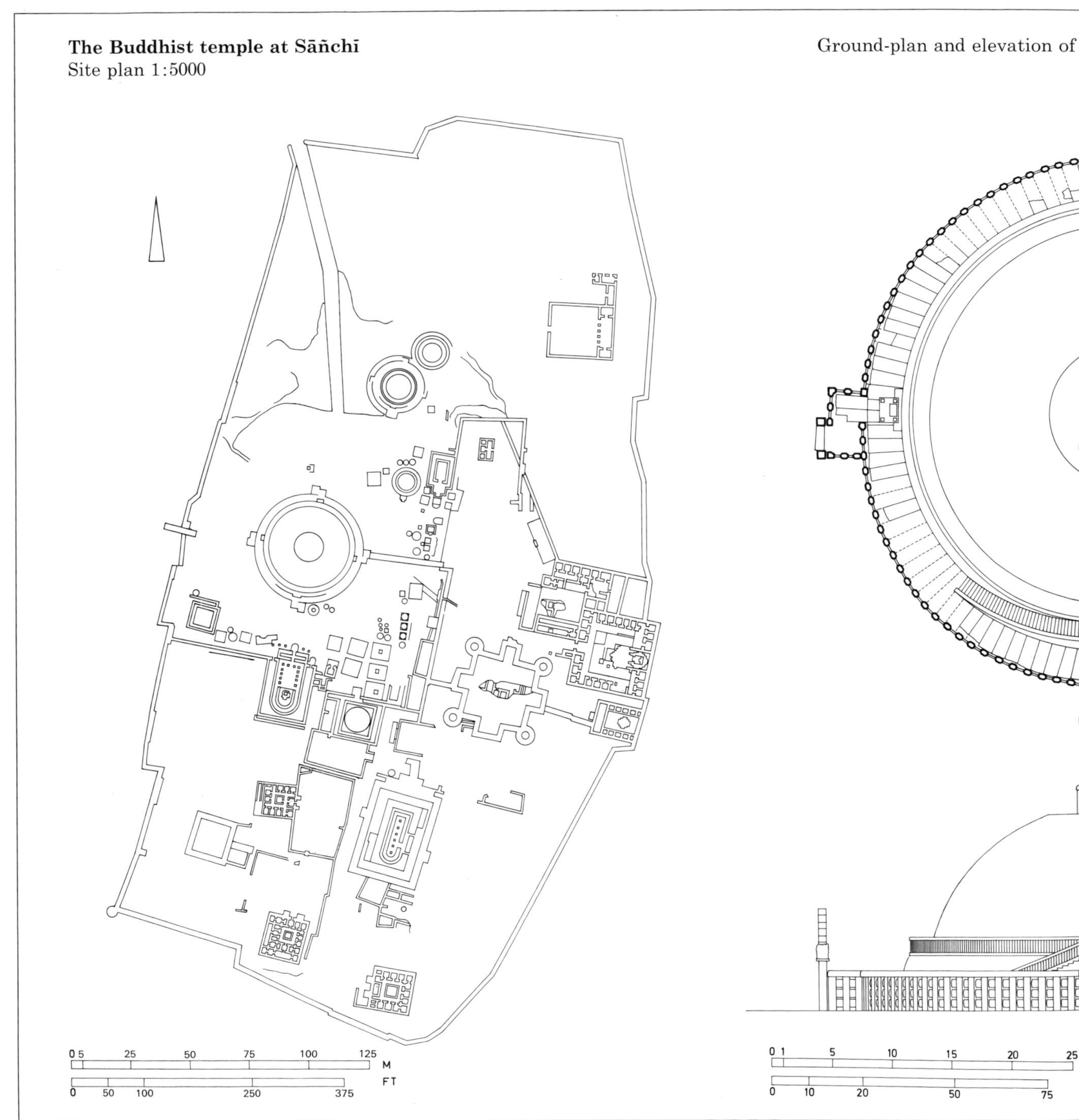
The Buddhist temple at Sāñchī
Site plan 1:5000
Ground-plan and elevation of
0 5 25 50 75 100 125 M
0 50 100 250 375 FT
0 1 5 10 15 20 25
0 10 20 50 75

…at Stūpa 1:500

Details of the balustrade 1:60 and the gateway 1:40

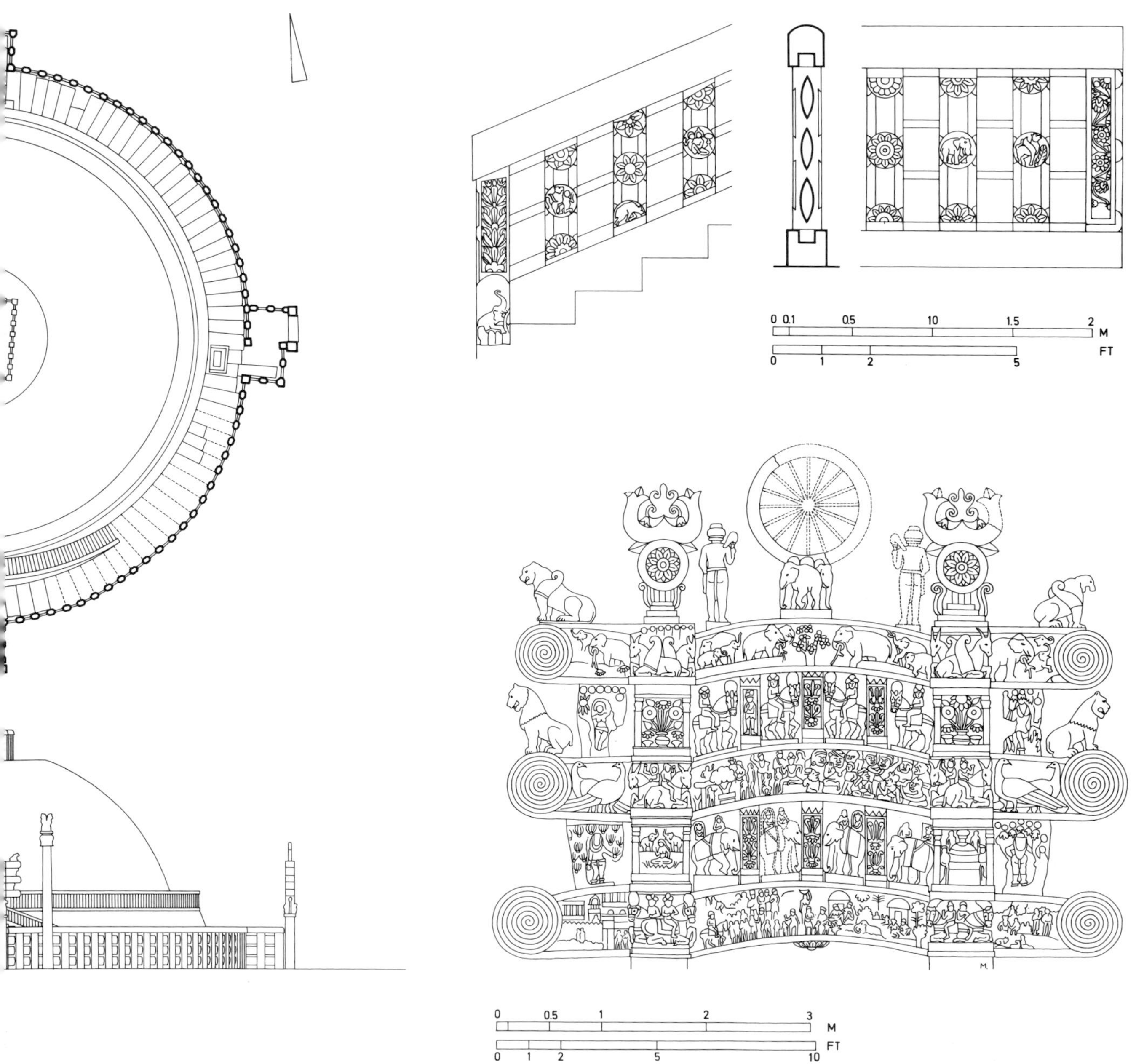

Notes

The Buddhist temples at Sāñchī

According to sacred tradition architecture and town planning experienced a period of greatness during the third century B.C. under the patronage of Ashoka, the first Buddhist emperor, but their glory is imperfectly reflected in very few archaeological finds. All the monuments were built of wood and clay: the wood rotted away, the clay crumbled from the force of the annual monsoon, the decorations of gold and precious stones fell into the hands of conquerors.

However, some burial mounds, whose external hemispherical forms were built of baked clay, have withstood the passage of centuries. For the Buddhist monks the shape of the Buddha's burial or relic mound became the symbol of his teaching. At the sacred places of India they built a countless number of these stūpas in brick or stone. In the monastery compound of Sāñchī a brick stūpa dating from the reign of Ashoka was expanded in the second century A.D. Taking over an old Aryan custom of surrounding sacred enclosures with a fence, the Buddhists surrounded the new stone stūpa with a splendid stone railing. The stūpa, originally a monument over the relics of the Buddha or of a saint, acquired a second meaning. It became a geometric image of Buddhist cosmology, oriented as precisely as possible towards the four cardinal points and with its measurements based on numerical symbolism. The most important motifs were the circle and the sphere, i.e. rounded forms symbolizing rotation.

The caves in the Barābar Hills

Buddhism spread out across the sub-continent from the capital and university cities of the Ganges plain. Missionary monks brought with them to southern and central India, in addition to the doctrine of the Enlightened One, contemporary north Indian types of building, such as the barrel roof of a bamboo hut or the domical roof of a wooden house. These types of building are often referred to as characteristically Buddhist, but they are only forms and structures which the Buddhists adopted from dwelling-houses. Thus the tradition of monolithic chaitya-halls begins with two caves, Lomas Rishi and Sudāma, dating from the middle of the third century B.C., which were carved, not by Buddhist monks, but by ascetics of the Ājīvika sect, from the granite of the Barābar Hills, about 50 kilometres from Bodh Gayā, an ancient Buddhist place of pilgrimage in the Ganges plain.

The prayer-hall at Kārlī

In the first century B.C. the development of Buddhist rock-cut architecture reached its zenith in the chaitya-hall of Kārlī. The architects usually sited their subterranean complexes of cult and dwelling chambers in remote valleys or on inaccessible rocky slopes. Near the modern town of Lonavala they carved the largest monolithic basilica in India on the top of a mountain. The work took several decades and was executed with very simple tools. In ground-plan and vertical section it is reminiscent of Christian basilicas, for the chamber had to meet similar ritual needs. The nave, the assembly hall of the priests, is oriented towards the cult object in the apse, the stūpa. The aisles, which were continued around the apse, were used for the circumambulation of the stūpa, a rite reminiscent of the processions in early Christian basilicas.

The monasteries of Ajantā

In all parts of India Buddhist monks preferred monolithic rock temples and monasteries to wooden or stone monuments. There were various reasons for the erection of such monolithic sanctuaries. Several advanced cultures in early times had subterranean temples connected with fertility and mother earth cults. But it is hard to explain why the monks took the trouble to execute their dwellings in the form of rock-cut architecture, since the monasteries were not conceived as defences but as costly edifices which enjoyed the patronage of pious rulers. Economic considerations were not predominant, although a comparison of the cost involved would show that monolithic subterranean monuments were not much more expensive than buildings of ashlar masonry.

The Buddhist chaitya-hall at Kārlī
Ground-plan and vertical section 1:500 and details of a pillar 1:80

1 Stūpa
2 Nave
3 Aisles
4 Vestibule

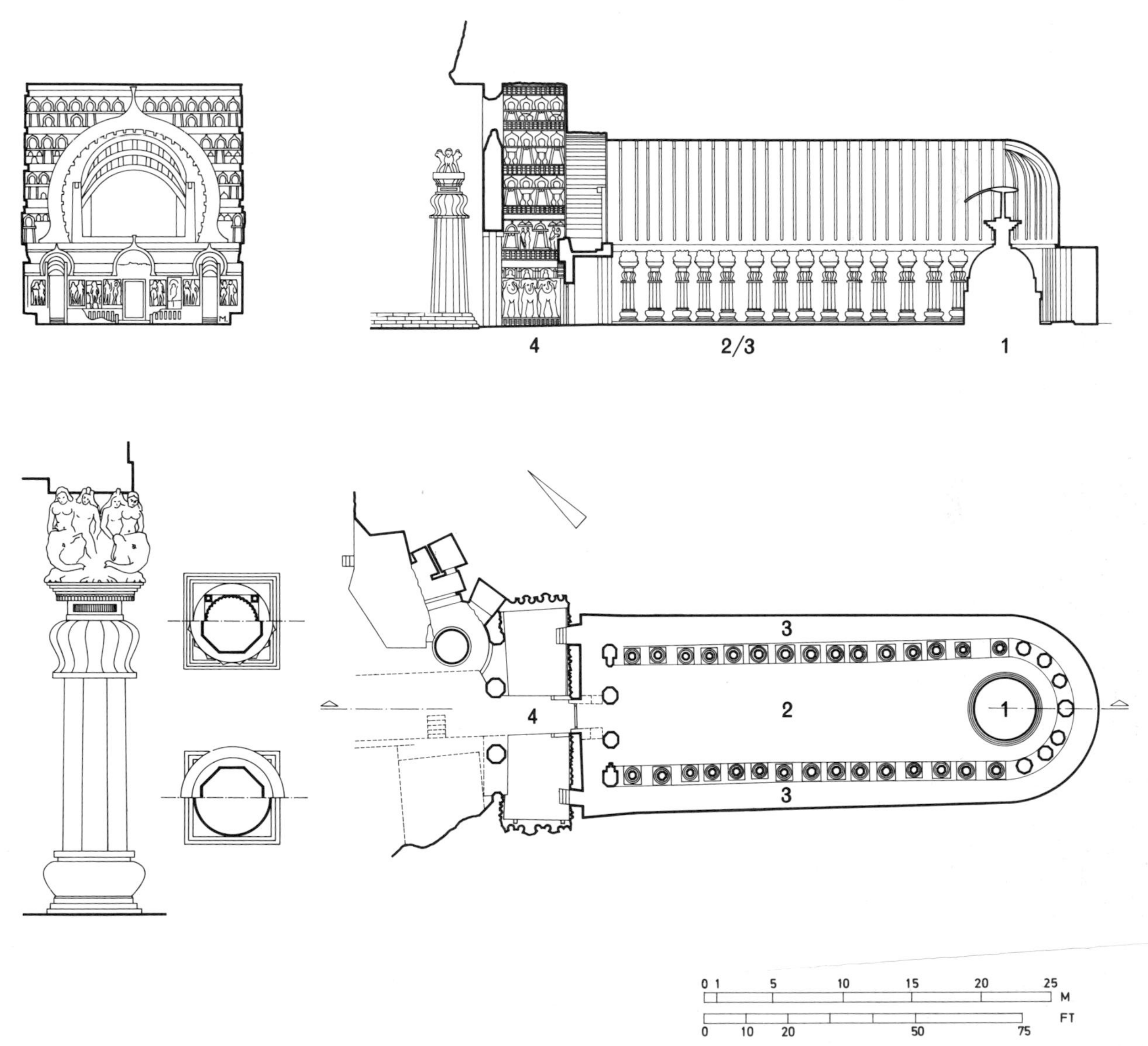

The Hindu Dharmarāja-ratha at Mahaballipuram
Elevation, vertical section, ground-plan and view from above 1:200

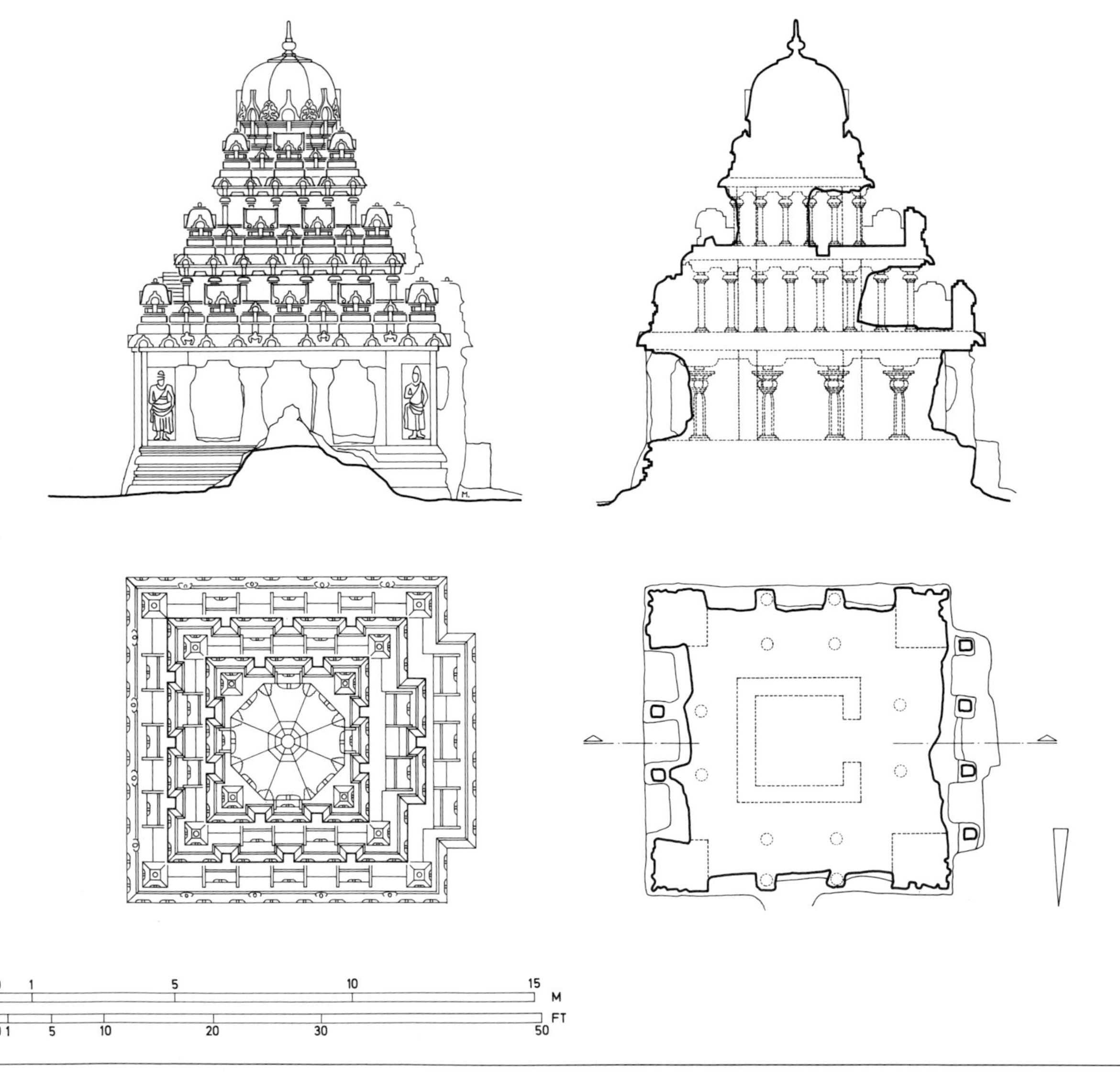

2. City and Temple Layout: The Vision of a Cosmic Plan

'Vāstu-vidyā', the science of architecture, was already a branch of occult knowledge in Vedic times. It was handed down orally from father to son. Not until the Middle Ages did it become necessary to put this knowledge down in writing. For during the flourishing period of temple-building the instructions relating to the rules of proportion became so numerous, and the ritual so complex, that it was no longer possible to avoid compiling manuals and reference works in which these instructions were laid down. The manuscripts relating to vāstu-vidyā, in most cases incised on palm-leaves which were then dried, are still today venerated in Hindu temples by the performance of a sacrificial rite. Only in rare instances have historians of architecture had the opportunity to analyse the form and structure of surviving buildings in the light of these original palm-leaf manuscripts. Even the nineteenth-century British authors of the 'Archaeological Survey of India' were obliged to confine themselves to recording and restoring abandoned temples.

In 1920 Stella Kramrisch made the first thorough effort to analyse the Hindu temples with the aid of several manuscripts, and to describe them from a viewpoint other than that of European commentators. During the decades that followed further manuscripts were discovered. These have only begun to be studied, and we still lack a comparison of the texts with the actual monuments.

In this chapter we shall deal with the symbolism implicit in Indian architecture. We shall see that the layout of a city is determined by the same principles of order as that of a temple or a house.

The vāstu-purusha mandala

In an ancient text it is stated: 'A long time ago something existed that was not defined by name or known in its form. It blocked the sky and the earth. When the gods saw it they seized it and pressed it upon the ground, face downwards. In throwing it to the ground, the gods held on to it. Brahmā had it occupied by the gods and called it "vāstu-purusha".'

Existence which as yet does not follow any principle is defined by Brahmā, who forces it to assume and retain a certain form, with the aid of the gods who are diffused over the vāstu-purusha. This story of the creation is of great significance in Indian architecture. The name given to form is 'mandala'. Thus the so-called vāstu-purusha mandala is the form assumed by existence, by the phenomenal world, now that it has been set in order. The geometric form of the vāstu-purusha mandala can be explained by reference to the Vedic sacrificial rite, during the performance of which the Aryans carried braziers from one altar to another. A round altar symbolizes the terrestrial world and a square one the celestial. A circular shape symbolizes movement, the cyclical movement of time. A square cannot be moved of itself, but is a final and unequivocal form. As perfect form, it is used by the Hindus to indicate the Absolute. If one considers the earth merely from its physical, external form it is depicted as a circle; if, however, it is regarded as the manifestation of the supreme principle, Brahman, it is rendered as a square, fixed by the cardinal points (points of the compass). Vāstu-purusha is thus pressed into the form of a square. In legends Purusha is also represented as a timid-looking old man, ugly and hunch-backed, and walking with a stoop. His crippled figure fills exactly one square. Each of the gods who keep him captive covers one quarter of his body. Wherever the symbol of vāstu-purusha is marked out on the ground, there he lies. The vāstu-purusha mandala is an image of the laws governing the cosmos, to which men are just as subject as is the earth on which they build. In their activity as builders men order their environment in the same way as once in the past Brahmā forced the undefined purusha into a geometric form.

The vāstu-purusha mandala, from an old Indian manual of architecture

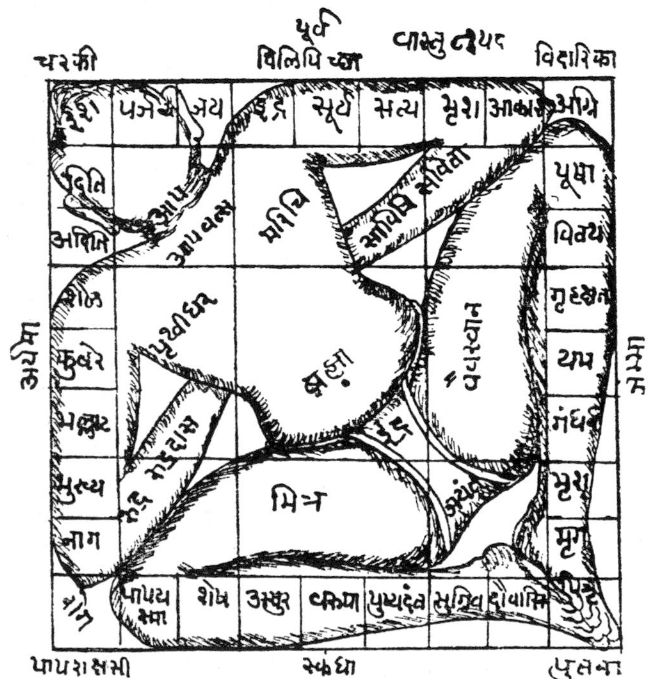

For the sthapati, building is an act of bringing disordered existence into conformity with the basic laws that govern it. This can only be achieved by making each monument, from the hermit's retreat to the layout of a city, follow exactly the magic diagram of the vāstu-purusha mandala.

All existence is reflected in this magic square. It is an image of the earth, which is a square derived from a circle; at the same time it is also the sacrificed body of the primeval being, Purusha. Man and earth correspond to one another in this image. Time enters the mandala by co-ordinating the signs of the zodiac, and space does so by orienting the square towards the four (or eight) cardinal points. The quarters or small squares, called 'pādas', which are covered by the individual gods, are grouped around a central Brahmā-sthāna comprising several such small squares. Important gods cover the innermost ring, and in the outer rings there follow the gods of lower rank in the celestial hierarchy. Strangely enough, the central square is no longer assigned to the 'unformed' Brahman, but expressly to the god Brahmā.

Purusha is also the personified cosmos, the superman who, according to legend, is manifested in sacrifice as the phenomenal world, the gods, the sun and

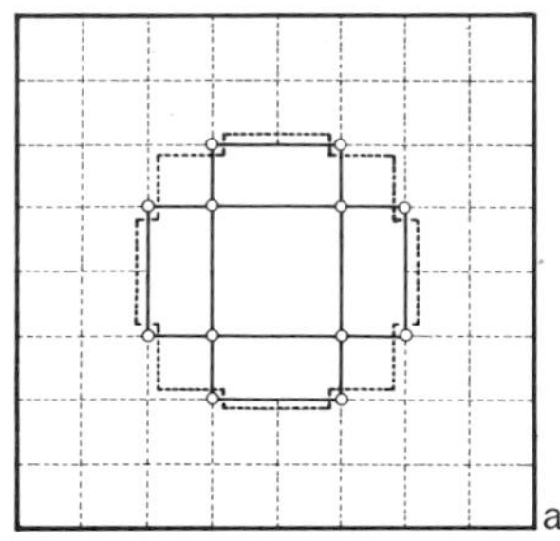
a)

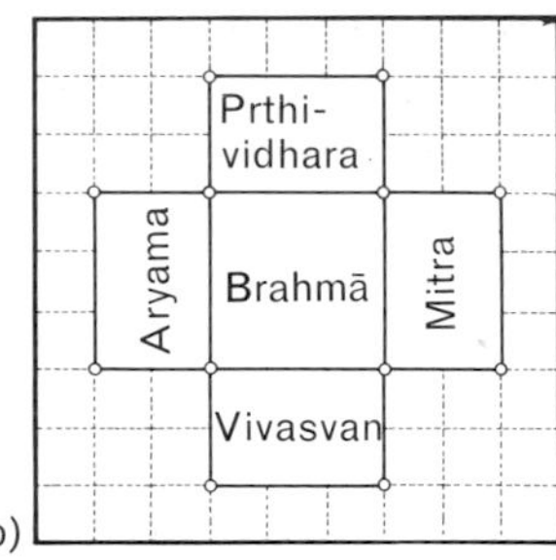

b)

a) The north Indian mandūka-mandala, containing 8 × 8 pādas. Around the central Brahmā-sthāna (4 units) are the pādas of the 'inner gods' (2 units) and the rings of the 'outer gods' (1 unit). The points of intersection (marmas) must not be interrupted by the lines of the ground-plan (shown here by thick lines)

b) The north Indian paramasayika-mandala, containing 9 × 9 pādas

moon, fire, air and earth. The idea of human sacrifice or of sacrifice in human guise is already known to the 'Vedas'. In the Aryan sacrificial rite a human being is represented symbolically in the arrangement of the sacrificial vessels. Three kettles form the head, two milk jars the ears, and so on. The erection of a Vedic sacrificial altar certainly did not presuppose human sacrifice, but the ritual and the symbols point to the fact that originally a sacrifice of this kind did indeed precede the erection of such an altar. From historical times we have testimony to the fact that the architect of a temple might be buried beneath its foundations, as a kind of sacrificial act.

According to the 'vāstu shāstras' (general manuals on architecture) the vāstu-purusha mandala can be drawn in 32 ways. The simplest one consists of a square; all the others result from the division of this square into 4, 9, 16, 25, 36, 49, 64, 81 and so on up to 1024 small squares, i.e. pādas. The size in which it is drawn is immaterial so far as its magic efficacy is concerned. In a plan for a large area it can regulate the disposition of the various buildings, and in the plan of a temple it can define the rhythm of the architectural members or the proportion between the thickness of the wall and the size of the interior.

The 'single-pāda mandala' is supposed to be taken as the plan for a hermit's retreat or for a small sacrificial hearth. In south Indian texts particular significance is attached to the mandala consisting of 7 × 7 pādas; but in all texts concerned with the doctrine of proportion there is general agreement that, of the numerous forms of mandala, two are of particular importance: the 'mandūka mandala', consisting of 64 pādas, and the 'paramasayika mandala', consisting of 81 pādas. The mandūka mandala is formed by dividing the sides of the squares into even numbers of parts. Its two central axes are oriented towards the cardinal points. The paramasayika mandala is formed by dividing the sides into uneven numbers of parts. The cardinal points can be directly co-ordinated with the eight pādas which constitute the central Brahmā-sthāna. In both kinds of mandala Brahmā is surrounded by 44 Vedic gods. As a rule four 'inner gods' cover the pādas bordering upon the Brahmā-sthāna; eight 'middle gods' cover the next ring; and finally 32 'outer gods' cover the pādas around the border. The vāstu-purusha mandala bears an external resemblance to an Indian horoscope. Even today Indian astrologers draw the zodiac in the form of a square divided into four parts in each direction, and enter the twelve signs of the zodiac in the twelve outer squares. In the vāstu-purusha mandala the ecliptic does not fit into twelve parts, so that usually the exterior ring of pādas is divided into 32 units which represent the 'lunar mansions'. This division is of no significance for the geometric composition of the mandala itself, but does play an important part in all astrological predictions about the circumstances in which building should be begun and continued. Each 'lunar mansion' coincides with one of the 32 gods of the outer ring. Eight of these gods – those in the corners and those in the middle of each side of the square – are considered to be guardians of the cardinal points, and determine the spatial orientation of the magic square.

We have to distinguish between two kinds of

purusha. In one of its manifestations, as a small image of the cosmos, it rotates on its own axis once a year, following the position of the sun in the ecliptic. The legs always point toward the sun, and the head is seven signs of the zodiac distant from it. The rotating purusha is supposed to serve as a metaphysical plan for all secular monuments. Temples, on the other hand, which as bodies of God are not subject to temporal laws in the same way, are erected on a vāstu-purusha mandala that is not envisaged as rotating.

The mandala in town planning

In the planning of a town or village one first has to ascertain which vāstu-purusha mandala is appropriate. Of the 32 possibilities the priest-astrologer chooses a mandala which on one hand seems astrologically most auspicious and which on the other hand has as many pādas as there are to be residential quarters. Once again, mandalas with 64 and with 81 pādas are held in particularly high regard.

So far as the natural features of its setting permit, the town is supposed to be an exact rectangle, if not actually a square, in outline. The town wall is erected along the outer border of the mandala. The streets run from north to south and from east to west along the lines marking off the pādas from one another. One dwelling block is exactly coextensive with one pāda. Detailed instructions about the network of streets are contained in one manuscript, which recommends the mandala with 64 pādas. Whether a city, a town or merely a market centre is planned, the following layout is provided for: a broad 'royal way' crosses the entire city, from north to south and also from east to west, following the median line of the diagram. In cities this royal way should be 12 metres wide, in towns 10 metres and in markets 8 metres. It should provide ample room for princely processions and also be wide enough for troops to march through with ease. The continuations of the royal way outside the four gateways ('gopura'), situated at the cardinal points, are used for communication with other cities and regions. Slightly narrower are the 'large carriage ways', of which a total of eight are included in the plan. In width they should measure six, five and four metres respectively. In this kind of street no pedestrians are allowed, as it is reserved for carriages and elephants. On the other hand, the narrowest streets, 'simple carriage ways', have separate footpaths on either side.

Along the inner side of the city wall the so-called 'processional way' runs continuously around the settlement. In its dimensions it is equal to the royal way. It is laid out on a grand scale, not only in order to facilitate deployment of troops in the case of an attack, but also in keeping with an ancient Aryan tradition: during the sacrificial rite the Vedic altar was venerated by being carried around clockwise in procession. Such sacred circumambulations were common in early Hinduism, whether the god being worshipped was originally a Vedic or a Dravidian one. The chief object of veneration was at first the sacrificial altar, and later the image or symbol of the god. Finally, in planned settlements, it was the invisible Brahmā-sthāna of the vāstu-purusha mandala.

Before any cities were founded the villages of the Aryan tribes were arranged as follows. In the centre there stood a huge tree, under which the elders held counsel and pronounced judgement. This tree symbolized the axis around which the universe and the celestial realms were believed to rotate. Its branches marked off the celestial worlds, superimposed one upon the other. The need to integrate even a small village harmoniously into the laws governing the cosmos meant that a path was made for the procession around the settlement, modelled on the symbolic processions with the altar; such a path was called a 'pradakshinā-patha'. The altar and the village are both images of the same supernatural order. In Hindu architecture the processional path determines the ground-plan of the sanctuary. In Buddhist architecture the circumambulation of the Buddha's burial mound, in the circular form typical of Buddhism (just as the rectangular form is typical of Hinduism), is one of the most important rites and has left its mark upon works of architecture.

The dwelling blocks produced by the division into pādas may be subdivided by alleys and footpaths in any sort of pattern. Only the main thoroughfares which give the city its basic aspect have to conform closely to the division of the vāstu-purusha mandala.

Orientation of the city in the surrounding terrain

In choosing the site for a new settlement, the first step is to ascertain to which of the three classical types of land the prospective building site belongs. 'Jangala' is the name given to barren land, situated far from water or rivers. Here the wind is hot and the soil black. 'Anupa' is attractive country, surrounded by rivers; the climate is refreshing and cool, the soil humid and fertile; there will be no shortage of fish or meat. Most stretches of terrain come under the category of 'Sadhāna'. Here everything is of average quality; the good and bad elements are intermingled.

The soil is now examined meticulously: its colour, smell, sound, feel and taste are taken into consideration. The colour of the soil indicates for which caste the site is particularly well suited. Four colours are distinguished: white, red, yellow and black. White soil is for Brahmins, red for Kshatriyas, yellow for Vaishyas, and black for Shūdras. Also the taste of the soil is linked to the caste system: sweet for Brahmins, astringent for Kshatriyas, pungent for Vaishyas, and bitter for Shūdras. One should avoid ground which, when struck, emits a sound resembling the howling of jackals, the barking of dogs, or the braying of donkeys.

Particular importance is attached to the fact that the land on which the town is to be built should slope toward the north or north-east. A southward slope brings death, a south-western one suffering. If a town is built on a western slope, the harvest will be threatened with destruction and the citizens with poverty; a north-western slope will lead to war. To build a town in a hollow is regarded as particularly dangerous and bound to lead to destruction. All these rules may seem absurd, but the last one at least shows that each rule stems from experience: anyone who has lived through a monsoon will appreciate at once why a hollow is an unsuitable place to build a settlement, for it would be transformed into a lake for several months of each year.

Whereas some manuals give approval to a square plan for the city, others point out that a square city ought properly to be inhabited by Brahmins alone. Other castes had no claim to such a perfect form, and had to live in rectangular towns. Distinctions of this kind were quite common during the early period of Aryan town planning. Each unit of the settlement was inhabited by members of a particular professional group. A dense network of country roads enabled goods to be transported with ease. In the ancient texts we find time and again such places as coach-makers' village, smiths' village, washermens' village, weavers' village, etc. This principle of reserving towns to certain professions was, however, abandoned when social and economic relationships became more complex, and men pursuing different trades became more interdependent. All manuals on town planning agree that a town in which professions and castes are mixed must have a plan based on the vāstu-purusha mandala. In its simplest form this plan can direct that Brahmins should live and work in the northern district, Kshatriyas in the eastern and south-eastern part, Vaishyas in the southern part and Shūdras in the western district. If this principle cannot be adhered to, then at least the residential block, or pāda, must be divided in such a way that the castes are clearly separated. Such subdivision of blocks is also required by another rule, which assigns various professions to a fixed place in the town. Goldsmiths, smiths and armourers are in principle only allowed to reside in the south-eastern part of the town; shepherds, herdsmen, fishermen and gaolers must live in the south-west; drivers and soldiers must reside in the west. The police headquarters and the municipal administration together with brandy distillers and wine merchants are assigned to the north-west. The residential quarters of Brahmins, astrologers and ascetics are in the northern part of the city; the north-east is taken up by markets and tradesmen's dwellings. The east is reserved for the palaces of royal or princely families, the court of the royal guard, and the offices of the leading civil servants.

The custom of reserving particular quarters of the town for certain castes is justified in manuals of architecture by reference to the image of the earth and the sky as 'Mount Meru': out of the infinite cosmic sea the phenomenal world rises up like a pyramid. The four triangles which form the pyramid are of different colours. The white triangle is the residence of Brahmins, the red one that of Kshatriyas, the yellow one that of Vaishyas, and the black one that of Shūdras.

Right up to the Moghul period most Indian cities were built of unbaked clay, wood and other highly perishable materials. Stone, the most durable material, was reserved for temples. Thus hardly any remains of urban complexes have survived, and it is not easy to judge how strictly the rules of the manuals were followed. From the eighteenth century, however, we know of the foundation of one city in north India which shows how strong this tradition was even under Moghul rule. The layout of this town, Jaipur in the Rājasthān district, corresponds to that prescribed in the ancient texts. But the individual monuments bear the distinct stamp of Moghul architecture, which spread outwards from Agra and Delhi. If we leave out of account one extension to the town on the eastern side, and the location of the town wall in the north-western corner (necessitated by the topography), its plan is as follows: a splendid avenue running from east to west, an incomplete street parallel to it, and the two main streets which run from north to south divide the city, which was originally rectangular in plan, into nine parts. (The extension to the south-east constitutes a tenth part.) The central area of the Brahmā-sthāna is reserved for the palace of the Mahārāja; the other blocks are subdivided more or less regularly by side streets and unpaved footpaths. The unsystematic division of the northern quarters of the town is due to the fact that the successors of the Mahārāja did not bother to keep to the plan when making their additions. Moreover, since one of them sold the Mahārāja's rich library as wrapping paper, no theoretical treatise has survived relating to this sole modern example of Hindu town planning.

Plan of the city of Jaipur

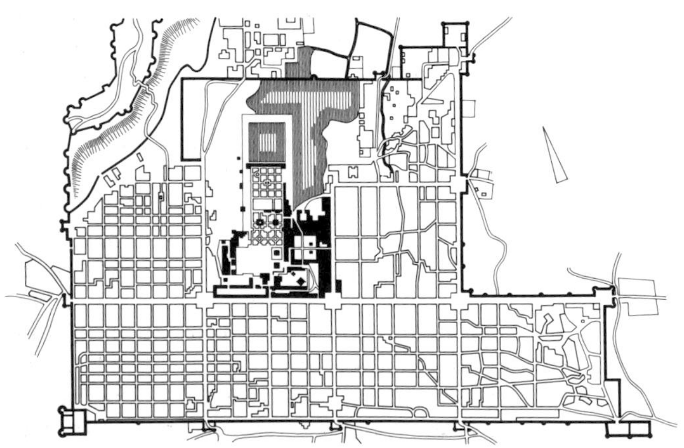

In Jaipur individual professional groups were allotted certain quarters of the town, wholly in accordance with the vāstu-vidyā. If one wants to find a cloth merchant even today, one must go to a particular street reserved for such persons. In another street all the bricklayers can be seen every morning, sitting in a long row on the pavement and waiting for someone to offer them employment. In another district one carpenter's shop adjoins another, and one basketmaker's shop another. This principle is taken to such lengths that today even bicycle shops are grouped together in this manner.

As the capital city of a temporal ruler, Jaipur is rectangular and not square in plan. Most of the buildings have the same number of storeys. As the city was evidently planned upon a vāstu-purusha mandala with unevenly divided sides, there is no central square. Particularly striking is the orientation: all the streets running in a longitudinal direction point east-south-east and west-north-west. Such a deviation from the cardinal points would not be remarkable, and might even be dismissed as an oversight, if the same deviation were not to be found in the orientation of the

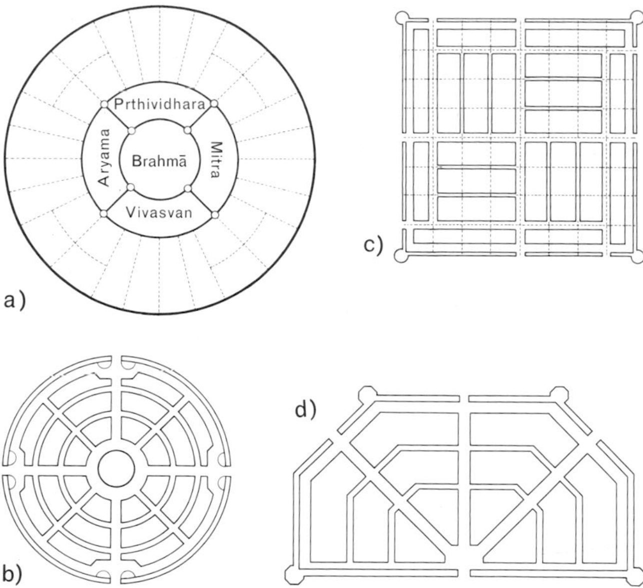

a) Circular vāstu-purusha mandala (manḋūka-mandala)
b) Sketch for a circular city based on a mandūka-mandala (after the Mānasāra)
c) Swastika plan for a city on a square mandūka-mandala
d) Kheta city for Shūdras

monumental astronomical observatory buildings, which are constructed exactly on an east-west and north-south alignment. Presumably this orientation of the town was necessitated either by the rules of proportion or by astrological considerations; for the site slopes toward the north-east, as the manuals direct, and this would have permitted a different orientation.

Besides the canonical alignment of the streets, following the lines marking off the pādas, the so-called swastika plan was no doubt also popular. The swastika, an ancient Aryan solar symbol, can be used in the ground-plan of a house, for the layout of the rooms, in town planning, to fix the sequence of the streets, and in a Buddhist stūpa, as an architectural symbol of the cyclical pattern through which all phenomena pass.

One variant of the normal town plan is the so-called 'kheta'. In the kheta towns only Shūdras were allowed to live. As a reflection of their imperfection this abbreviated plan has no proper centre. The optical centre is a point on the town wall, whereas its focal point in the plane is of no importance.

The building site

On a day fixed by the astronomers, the priest-architects charged with planning the town go to the tract of land selected. They determine the cardinal points by erecting in the middle of the site a column which tapers towards the top. Around its base they draw a circle with a radius twice the height of the column. At sunrise the shadow of the gnomon is longer than the radius of the circle. When during the morning the shadow of the tip of the column strikes the outline of the circle, the point of intersection is marked. In the afternoon the shadow lengthens again. The second point of intersection with the circle is then marked and linked with the first one, and the line between them points east and west. A parallel line through the centre of the circle indicates the east-west axis of the town. The north-south axis is determined by drawing two circles to give a median vertical line.

The outer line of the vāstu-purusha mandala is now marked out and its corners indicated by pegs. The entire terrain, i.e. the vāstu-purusha mandala, is levelled so that the building site corresponds as exactly as possible to the concept of a flat square world. At a favourable moment the priest-architect makes a sacrificial offering of fried rice and white flowers. After ritually cleansing himself by sacred ablutions, he ploughs a furrow along the east-west axis of the city using a plough made especially for the purpose. Then a group of Shūdras ploughs the entire terrain and sows various kinds of corn. When the corn is ripe the prospective inhabitants of the town, accompanied by the priest, again make their way to the building site. On this occasion they take with them all the cattle belonging to the community and allow them to eat the harvest. 'After two nights,' we are told, 'the terrain is cleansed by the grazing of the livestock, consecrated by the breathing of the cows and the lowing of the oxen, sanctified by the saliva from the mouths of the calves, washed by their urine, smeared with their mire and chewed fodder, and marked by their hooves.' On the ground so cleansed and sanctified the vāstu-purusha mandala with all its pādas can now be drawn.

The temple plan

The areas allotted in the plan for temples are once again cleansed from demons and earth spirits by the same rite before building commences. The size of the new vāstu-purusha mandala is not open to determination by the architect, since a number of requirements about its proportions have to be complied with. In considering Indian rules of proportion, we are not concerned only with the relationship between two or more architectural members. The Indian doctrine of proportion is designed not only to correlate the various parts of a temple in an aesthetically pleasing manner, but also to bring the entire building into a magical harmony with time and space, as well as with the caste of the builder. True, in all manuscripts the proportion between the length, breadth and height of the various parts is the subject of detailed, hardly comprehensible rules, but the central element in the doctrine is that each temple must correspond to six magical prerequisites.

Absolute perfection is the characteristic of Brahman, whereas the essence of the phenomenal world is imperfection. In mathematics imperfection is reflected, as the sthapati sees it, in fractions whose sum does not produce a whole number, but leaves a remainder which through further division yields the parts after the decimal point. In making such divisions the Indians use in their calculations only the integer, and regard the remainder as the most important result of the whole arithmetical operation. Thus in Indian architecture the doctrine of proportion is, strictly speaking, a 'doctrine of the remainder'. In working out fractions the sthapati is concerned not with the final result but instead with the remainder; it is this that has to conform to the rules of proportion.

Thus, for example, one is supposed to multiply the width of a temple by three and then divide it by eight (here the eight possible directions in which a building may be oriented enter into the calculation). The remainder from this sum, called 'yoni', indicates the cardinal point towards which the temple should be oriented. The cardinal points, starting with zero and ending with seven, are numbered clockwise. A yoni of zero is favoured, i.e. an orientation towards the east. Also four is an acceptable yoni, for this gives an orientation towards the west. Any other yoni would spell misfortune. The calculation must be carried out by varying the prospective width of the temple until a remainder of four, or better still zero, is obtained.

The width of a temple must, however, also conform to a different calculation, according to which the remainder is called 'vyaya'. The calculation made to determine the vyaya is as follows: $\frac{\text{width} \times 9}{10}$. Now the length of the temple is determined by the 27 planets. $\frac{\text{Length} \times 8}{27}$ yields the remainder 'rksha' and determines the star under which the temple must be built. If the temple is to be built under a particular star, its length must be adjusted until the index number of the star is obtained as remainder. But at the same time one must also satisfy a formula which takes into account the signs of the zodiac: $\frac{\text{Length} \times 8}{12}$. Its remainder, called 'āya', should if possible be zero. Finally, the length and width of the temple are tested together in two further formulae. These relate to the circumference of the temple. $\frac{\text{Circumference} \times 9}{7}$ yields the remainder 'vāra'. The seven in the denominator stands for the seven days in the week. The remainder vāra fixes the day of the week on which the building of the temple must be commenced, so that it is in keeping with the cyclical chronology. Time is also expressed in the measurements of the temple by the following calculation: $\frac{\text{Circumference} \times 9}{30}$ yields the remainder 'tithi'. Tithi fixes which one of the 30 lunar days is propitious for the commencement of the building.

To fulfil all these requirements is very difficult, since it is not the six equations with their six unknown quantities, but the incalculable remainder of a division sum that is always the decisive factor.

In addition to these six basic requirements governing the proportions, two further calculations should if possible be carried out. These relate to the caste of the donor and the length of time that the temple is designed to last. $\frac{\text{Length} \times \text{width} \times 9}{4}$ gives the caste; $\frac{\text{length} \times \text{width} \times 27}{100}$ gives the duration of the building. If one assumes, for example, that a temple measures 11 cubits in length and five cubits in width, the duration of the temple will be as follows:
$\frac{5 \times 11 \times 27}{100} = 1485:100 = 14$; remainder 85 – i.e., the temple will stand for 85 years. The caste of the donor is found as follows: $\frac{5 \times 11 \times 9}{4} = 495:4 = 123$; remainder 3. This means that a temple of these dimensions may only be founded by a peasant or craftsman. The week-day on which building may commence is found as follows:

$$\frac{(5+5+11+11) \times 9}{7} = 288:7 = 41;\ \text{remainder } 1.$$

Thus building may begin only on a Monday. The orientation of the temple is found as follows:
$\frac{5 \times 3}{8} = 15:8 = 1$; remainder 7. A temple with these dimensions thus has to be oriented toward the north-east. But this is not auspicious, for the remainder ought to be zero (east) or at least four (west). Therefore before one could calculate the lunar day or the planet under which this temple should be built, one would have to begin the calculation all over again with different dimensions. Another complicating factor is that the calculated lunar day must finally concide with the calculated week-day and, last but not least, with a favourable constellation. If all these requirements are impossible to co-ordinate, the construction of the temple has to be postponed or completely abandoned.

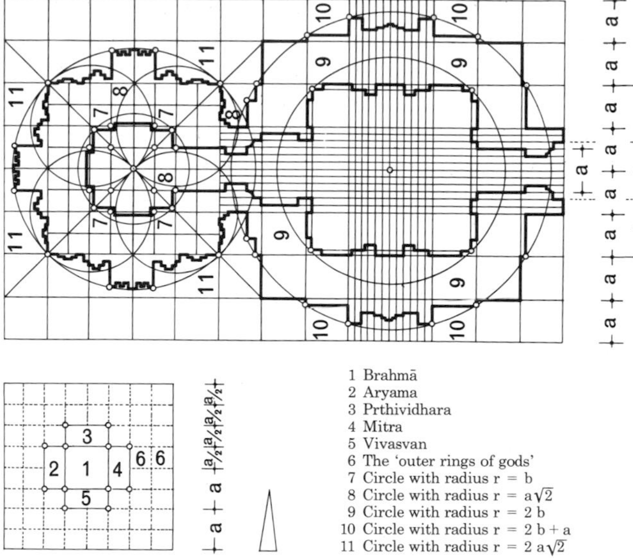

The Brahmeshvara temple at Bhuvaneshvar, its grid and the proportions resulting from it. (Detail from the general layout; see also plan p. 151)

Early temples in north India consisted only of the sanctuary, or 'garbha-griha' (literally, womb). This narrow cubic cella is enclosed within thick walls. From the eighth century A.D. onwards, in addition to this tower, a second independent architectural member is to be found: an assembly hall, the so-called 'mukhashālā', erected for believers in front of the cella. In contrast, the mukhashālā is a spacious room, enclosed within thin walls. It is provided with sufficient lighting by the entrance in the east and two additional windows along the north-south axis. The west door leads to the dark sanctuary.

The Brahmeshvara temple at Bhuvaneshvar, for example, follows this classical disposition (see plan, p. 151). A photograph of the building shows that the walled platform which supports the temple with its four ancillary shrines was divided in a certain proportion. All architectural members are incorporated systematically into a fixed network of lines. The platform is divided into 14 × 21 squares, each with sides measuring approximately 1.51 metres. The point of intersection of two diagonal lines, leading from the south-western and north-western corners of the platform, determines the ritual centre of the building, the point above which Shiva's symbol, the phallus or 'lingam', is erected. The cella around the lingam affords just enough room for ritual circumambulation; the walls are devoid of any decoration. The mandala, containing 4 × 4 pādas, is laid out around this centre. By dividing these squares one obtains the mandūka mandala, comprising 8 × 8 pādas. Its corners are at the same time the corners of the external outline of the cella. To the east of the garbha-griha is the mukhashālā, which follows its own rules of proportion. In the interior it is exactly as wide as the exterior of the garbha-griha; its wall is as thick as one square in the plan. The vāstu-purusha mandala of the garbha-griha is separated from the outline of the mukhashālā, with its 6 × 6 pādas, by a strip one plan unit broad. Here the architect has had to master the difficult problem of effecting the transition between the two parts of the building. In many temples a small intermediate space is left at this point. But the architect of the Brahmeshvara temple has chosen a different solution. The garbha-griha and the mukhashālā have extensions like passages, which meet at the deeply recessed splayed door which gives access to the cella.

There is, however, no optical link between the two chambers. Both the cella and the assembly hall have, in addition to their common east-west axis, a symmetrical axis from north to south. Here the believer is not, as in Buddhist prayer-halls, led consciously to the centre. In temple architecture, too, a difference is made (one which rules out all comparisons) between the area representing the phenomenal world, with all its profusion of forms, and the 'womb' of the temple, with its simplicity and lack of ornamentation; the latter is not an attempt to represent the body of the deity, let alone to illustrate the supreme formless Self, the Brahman – for the tower of the temple 'is' God, not merely his abode.

For some reason still unknown the structure of the mukhashālā is based both upon a division of the interior into four parts, covering 16 squares in the plan, and upon a division into three parts. Three parts 'b' correspond to four parts 'a'. The smallest unit of measurement, which appears time and again in the ground-plan, is thus one-sixth of 'a' or one-eighth of 'b'; consequently, 1 'b' = $1^1/_3$ 'a'.

The vāstu-purusha mandala of the garbha-griha does not tally exactly with the ground-plan. In medieval treatises on the relationship between the mandala and the building one finds an explanation of

The development of the ground-plan of the north Indian cella
a) 3-ratha type (triratha)
b) 5-ratha type (pañcharatha)
c) further development of the 5-ratha type
d) 7-ratha type (saptaratha)

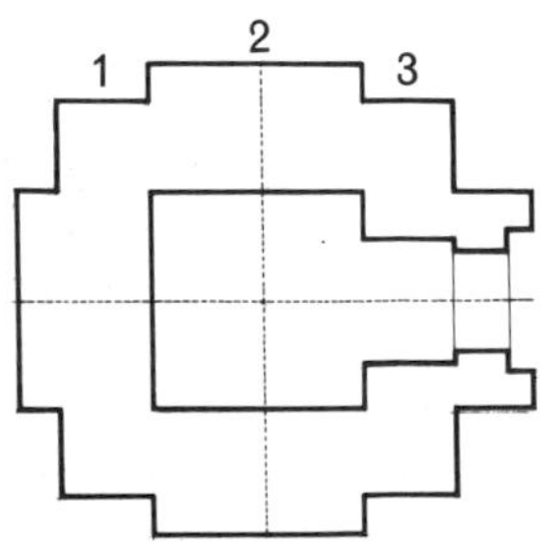

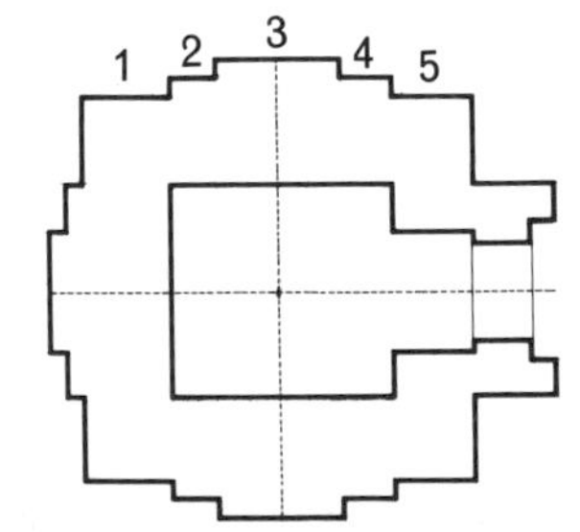

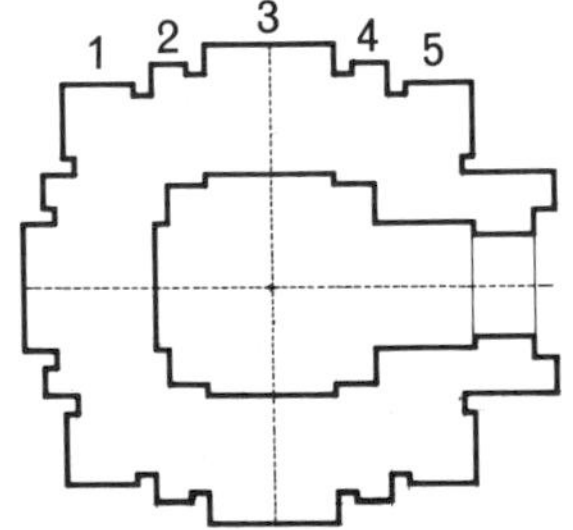

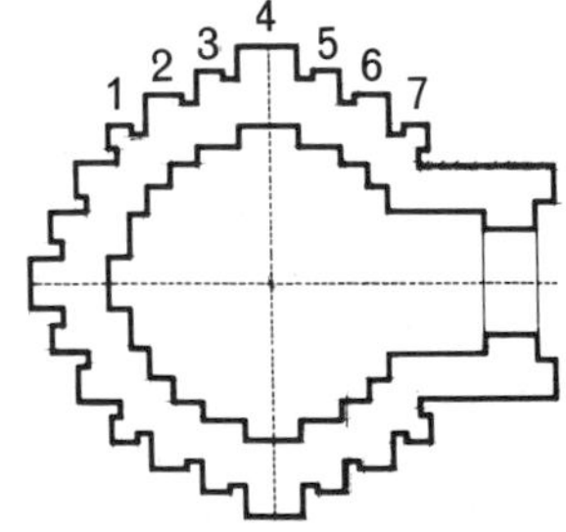

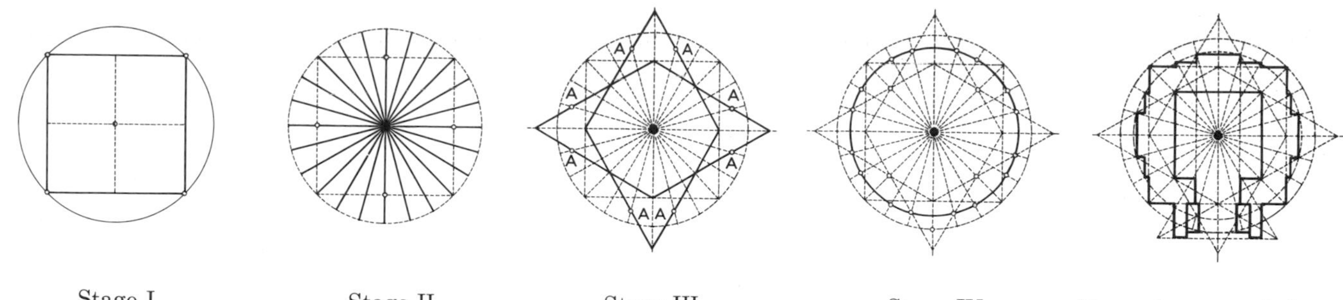

Stage I Stage II Stage III Stage IV

Development of the ground-plan of a temple from the square and the chronological division of the circle

Example: ground-plan of an ancillary shrine of the Brahmeshvara temple at Bhuvaneshvar

this fact. The Brahmā-sthāna is separated from the surrounding four 'inner gods' by the lines of the vāstu-purusha mandala. In the conception of the priest-architect these lines extend three-dimensionally, even though they are drawn as no more than thin lines on the foundations of the temple. Above all, the points at which the magic lines of force intersect are to be regarded as three-dimensional. The points of intersection ('marmas') around the Brahmā-sthāna are especially sacred, as are those marmas which form the corners of the 'inner' pādas. The further the dividing lines between the pādas – or the marmas – are from the centre, the less sensitive and important they are in regard to the magic efficacy of the mandala. In any case the architect must avoid damaging the marmas in the centre, around the Brahmā-sthāna and the 'inner' pādas, by interrupting them with wall salients, columns or other architectural members. And yet the interior of the cella ought to tally with the Brahmā-sthāna so far as is possible. The general rule is that the three-dimensional extension of the marmas runs to one-eighth the length of the side of a pāda. The walls of the cella have to be adjusted by this amount. So that the cella's dimensions should not be arbitrarily determined, the architect chooses a form that has already been fixed, namely 'b', a half-diagonal of the garbha-griha. Thus it is slightly smaller than the Brahmā-sthāna, and the marmas, not encroached upon by the lines of the ground-plan, extend one-eighth the side of a pāda within the masonry. Also the niches, which in the stone cella were taken over from those in earlier wooden buildings, are given proportions which avoid the marmas.

The evolution of the outer contour of a north Indian temple tower is chiefly based upon the square. From the need to erect cult images of the guardians above each of the cardinal points the custom developed, as early as the time when temples were built of wood, of adding niches axially, outside the actual body of the building. From this evolved the simplest ground-plan of the temples that have survived, the so-called 'ratha' type. Rathas or 'pāgas' are vertical salients or recesses of walls; three rathas are made in the façade of the garbha-griha by bringing forward three sections of the wall, of the same width as the interior, to accommodate an external niche. In the classical period architects were no longer content with this simple articulation of the façade. The next step was to divide the sides of the square into five parts. So we get the most common of all ground-plans: the five-ratha type. The depth of the ratha salients and recesses can be determined by various geometrical operations. Usually the rathas are the same width and project outwards to the same extent. In the case of the Brahmeshvara temple we do not yet know the geometrical construction of the rathas, which are themselves lavishly articulated. All that is certain is that the axial rathas project so far that they terminate in a circle, drawn around the square of the vāstu-purusha mandala or garbha-griha.

The research carried out by Alice Boner has shown that the sculptures in Shiva temples are usually based on a segment of a circle measuring 15 degrees. The outlines of the four small ancillary shrines in the Brahmeshvara temple, dedicated to various manifestations of Shiva, seem to be constructed in a similar way. All the projecting corners of the rathas are located on one of the 24 diameters of a 15-degree segment.

Let us now reconstruct step by step the geometric composition of one of these ancillary shrines, following the sequence in which a sthapati would have drawn the lines on the temple platform. The four plan squares that were allotted at each corner of the platform to ancillary shrines form the square on which the ground-plan is based. This square is the world, fixed by the cardinal points and extending between the four corners: north-west, north-east, south-east and south-west. Its chronological aspect is rendered in the form of a circle, which circumscribes the temple; this is divided into 12 or 24 segments which represent chronological divisions. Equilateral triangles erected over the axes have sides that are the same length as those of the square. The points 'A' where the triangles intersect the radii of the circle form the outer corners of the axial rathas. A second circle is drawn around the centre of the cella but this

Top: palm-leaf manuscript in original size
Left: portrait of the architect with surveyor's rod and triangle
Right: calculations of proportions

Bottom: reverse side of the same palm-leaf
Left: vertical section of a temple tower with indications of heights
Right: the mandala, on the basis of which the architect can freely compose the ground-plan

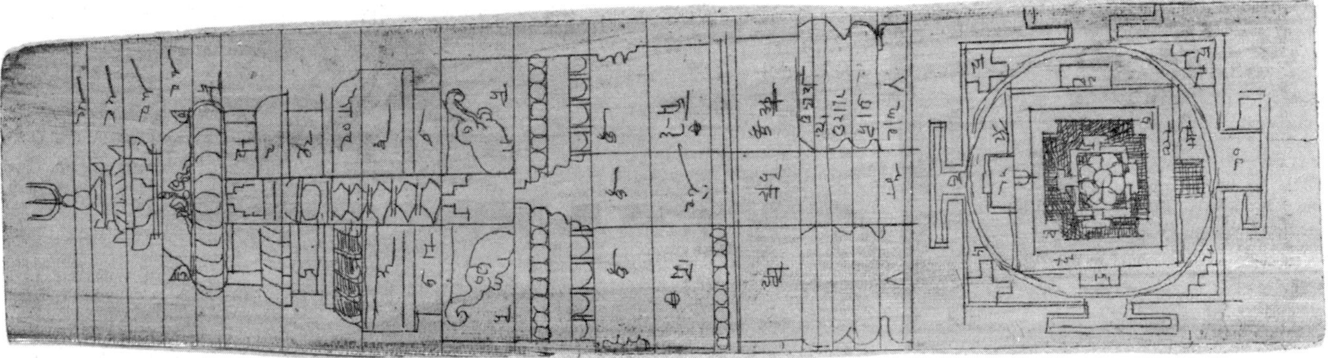

time runs through the corners; the points where this circle intersects the radii determines the location of the central ratha. The outer rathas, called 'konaka rathas', meet at the remaining radii. Thus each radius of the 15-degree segment has its function in the ground-plan. Four of them locate the shrine in relation to the cardinal points; four others form the diagonals of the basic square; and the remaining 16 determine the width and depth of the rathas. The distance between the corner points of the central rathas is equal to the exterior width of the door on the entrance side. The outer limit of the threshold is defined by a tangent of the basic circle and the inner limit by the basic square. The opening in the wall behind the entrance door is as broad as the axial rathas. Finally, the points where the triangles over the basic square intersect with the segmentation of the circle also define the projection of the 'entrance ratha'.

It is not difficult to find the geometric key to a ground-plan. But when it is a matter of interpreting the esoteric content of these graphic constructions and formulae we are unfortunately reduced to conjectures.

The structure of the entrance door is also subject to exact rules. The opening is always supposed to be twice as wide as that of the stone door jamb. The architects of the temples at Orissā kept to these proportions as a matter of general principle; only in the case of very small shrines – such as we find all around the Brahmeshvara temple – did they have to enlarge the opening by the width of one door jamb, as otherwise the entrance would have been too narrow. The opening ought to be twice as high as it is wide and as deep as it is broad. The entrance to the main temple conforms exactly to these requirements, as do the doors giving access to the ancillary shrines.

Now that we have considered the ground-plan of the Brahmeshvara temple, as an example of the type of temple found in north India, we can turn to the ground-plan of a south Indian temple. We shall choose the sanctuary at Tanjore which was donated by the Chola king Rāja-rāja in 1010 to commemorate the

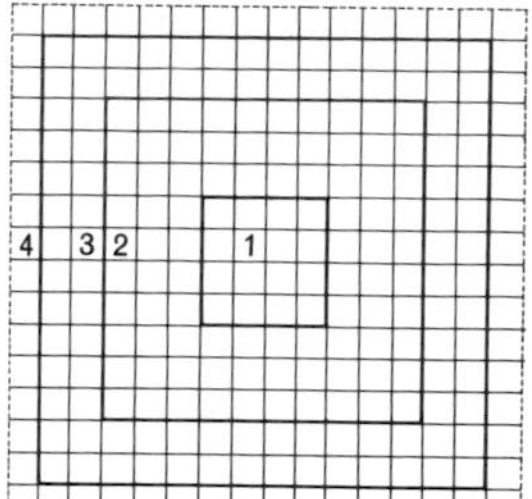

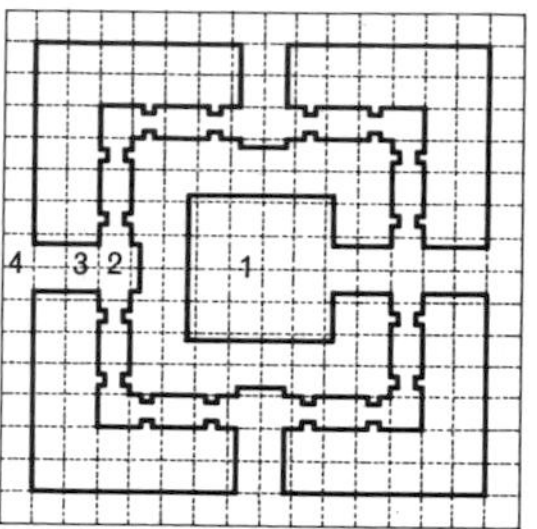

1) Brahmā	=	1) Sanctuary (garbha-griha) with interior pradakshinā-patha
2) Spheres of the gods	=	2) Circumambulatory path (exterior pradakshinā-patha)
3) Sphere of humans	=	3) Circuit wall
4) Sphere of demons	=	4) Terrace

The south Indian padmagarbha-mandala and the cella at Tanjore have the same geometrical divisions

victories he had won over neighbouring kingdoms. A strong wall encloses the temple compound, which once again is situated within a fortified area. The orientation of this fort and of the temple is determined by the course of a river flowing to the south of the defensive walls. In the orientation of the temple there is a considerable deviation from the east-west axis. As with the Brahmeshvara temple, the cella is located at the point of intersection of two diagonals (see plan, p. 151). The square formed by these diagonals is divided into nine smaller squares. Within the one in the centre a circle is then drawn, and within this circle a square. This square defines the limits of the raised platform which serves as a foundation for the cella. On this plane the mandala is drawn.

A south Indian mandala differs from the vāstu-purusha mandala described in north Indian manuals. South Indian sthapatis were not familiar with the legend according to which disordered Being was confined by Brahmā within the orderly form of a mandala, nor with the version according to which Purusha, the hunch-backed primeval man (who is at the same time a demon and the cosmos) lies on his stomach under the site of every building. Instead, the sthapati draws a magic sign, which is outwardly similar but has a different significance, upon the foundations of the temple or upon the tract of land where a new town is to be built. He visualizes the cosmic order as follows: the centre and essence of all Being is Brahmā (presumably originally the 'non-created Brahman'); around this, in a ring, is the world of the gods. At a greater distance from Brahmā, in contact with him only through the realm of the gods, and forming an outer ring around these gods, are the terrestrial phenomena, the world of human beings. At the bottom of this hierarchy are the goblins, demons and spirits. These have no contact with the gods or with Brahmā, and inhabit the fringe of the realms arranged concentrically around Brahmā.

The south Indian temple city of Shrīrangam is an image of the worlds situated in concentric rings around Brahman

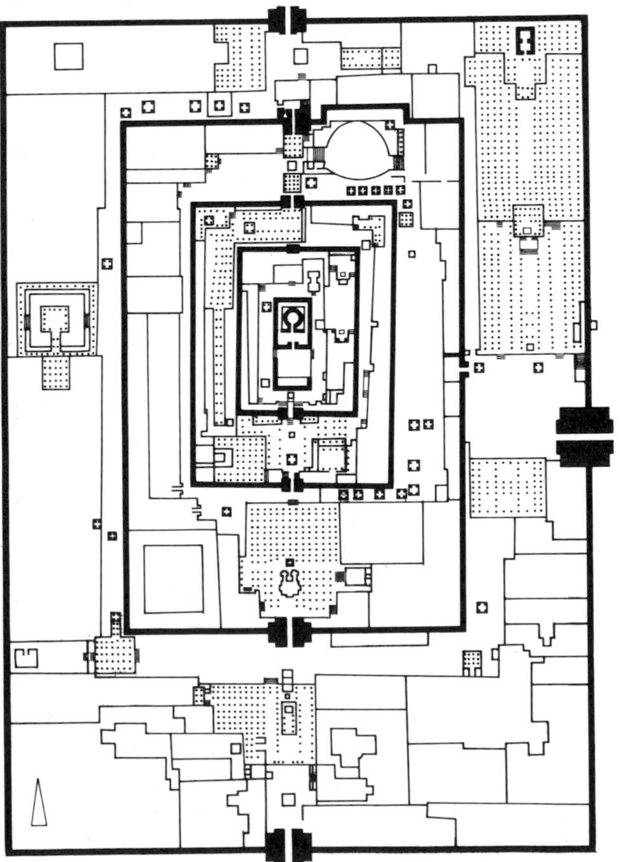

The graphic rendering of this cosmic plan, the so-called 'sthandila mandala', determines the spatial arrangement of the south Indian temple. Once again there are several designs, the most important of which is the mandala comprising 49 panels. Besides this sthandila mandala, the south Indian texts refer to the 'padmagarbha mandala'. Of its 16 × 16 panels, 16 are reserved for the Brahmā-sthāna, 84 for the ring of gods, 96 for that of the terrestrial world, and 60 for the narrow ring of demons and spirits. This padmagarbha mandala forms the structural plan of the cella at Tanjore.

The 16 panels of the Brahmā-sthāna tally with the interior of the cella; but, as in the case of the ground-plans of north Indian temples, the wall is not erected exactly upon the line of the mandala, but is adjusted in such a way that it does not touch the marmas, in their three-dimensional extension. The wall of the cella and the gallery for processional circumambulation fill the ring of the pantheon; the wall is two pādas thick and the gallery one pāda wide. Above the terrestrial world rises the outer wall of the cella, which is two pādas thick. For the realm of spirits and demons there is no room in the sanctuary. They are allotted the width of that part of the foundation which projects outside the building, far from the sacred lingam of Shiva in the Brahmā-sthāna.

The open halls ('mandapa') of the cella and the small shrines within the circuit walls of the sanctuary are not incorporated in the original plan. They are the work of later generations, when the occult system of dividing the plane had already been forgotten.

The extent to which the application of a south Indian mandala is fixed can be seen from the site plans of temple cities in this part of the country. In a typical town of this kind the temple is not separated by a circuit wall from the residential and business quarter nearby, but instead one finds several rings of streets around the cella. The innermost ring is bordered on

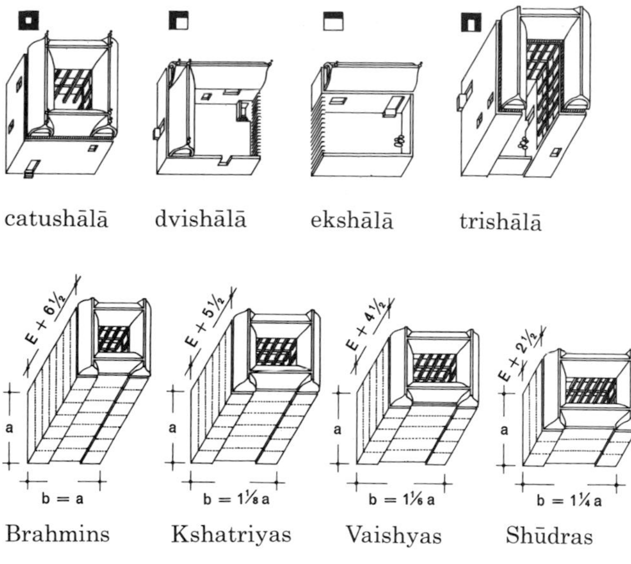

The ancient Indian dwelling-house was supposed to indicate by its proportions the caste of the owner

either side by ancillary shrines and prayer-halls. In the second ring are the dwellings of priests and a number of stalls where frankincense, flowers and fruit are sold for the 'pūjā' sacrifice. The further one moves away from the cella, the less sacred is the area. In the outer streets of temples, normal business activity sets the tone. This town plan conforms to the concept of the cosmos as arranged in concentric rings around Brahman. Although the tower above the relatively small cella is gilded, it is quite inconspicuous. In the cardinal points of the ring walls, marking off the different areas, are splendid porch or gate towers known as 'gopura'.

Brahman, the incognizable centre of Being, cannot be featured in the mandala of a temple city, since it is attributeless. The realms of the gods, on the other hand, are not beyond man's imaginative power and thus also of his ability to render them. But it is only in the rings of the terrestrial and demon worlds that all the exuberance and splendour of earthly things can testify to the power of Brahman. In the temple city of Shrīrangam this principle is clearly expressed in the alignment of the circular walls and in the porch towers, which increase in height as one approaches the exterior. The temple city of Madurai has much the same plan, but it has been repeatedly enlarged and modified by successive ruling dynasties, and so has lost its original precise layout. Paradoxically enough, the temple complex at Madurai contains two cellas dedicated to different gods. This makes it impossible for the zones representing the various worlds to be arranged in an orthodox circular form around a single centre.

The need to keep all mandalas secret was motivated in the ancient manuals by the argument that only experienced persons would know how to utilize properly the magic force obtainable from the symbols. Much mischief could be brought about by someone who abused the mandala. The mandala is also called 'yantram' (instrument), a term denoting an instrument used for observing the stars.

The town house

The caste stratification of Hindu society is reflected not only in the ground-plan of a city but also in its vertical section. The rules pertaining to the number of storeys permitted in dwelling-houses make it easy to ascertain which caste the proprietor belongs to. Thus a Shūdra is not allowed to build higher than GF + $2^{1}/_{2}$ (GF = ground floor) and a Vaishya up to GF + 4. Kshatriyas can build houses up to GF + $5^{1}/_{2}$ and Brahmins up to GF + $6^{1}/_{2}$. Finally, kings may build their palaces one storey higher still.

The main entrance of a dwelling, unlike that of a temple, is supposed never to be sited axially; the way it is oriented depends upon the caste of the builder. Wherever a house is located in the city district, the entrance door must be on the south side if the householder is a Brahmin, on the west if he is a Kshatriya, on the north if he is a Vaishya, and on the east if he is a Shūdra. The square of the vāstu-purusha mandala is taken as the basis for the residence of a Brahmin. It is the perfect form, appropriate only for those close to the gods. For this reason the ground-plan of a Brahmin house must not deviate from the square by more than one-tenth the length of a side. In clearly defined deviations from this absolute standard, the proportion of the sides in a Kshatriya house must be $1:1^{1}/_{8}$; of a Vaishya house $1:1^{1}/_{6}$; and of a Shūdra house $1:1^{1}/_{4}$.

The most popular ground-plan is the 'catushālā', in which the inner court is enclosed on all four sides by buildings. All the rooms open on to the court, and galleries afford communication between them. With this type of house several storeys can be built within a closely confined space, for the shadow cast upon the court by the buildings is welcome, and the rooms on the lower storeys are pleasantly cool. The outer walls facing the street do not have any windows, for reasons of security. With this symmetrical ground-plan the location of the entrance to the house presents no problem, even though it has to face a particular cardinal point in accordance with the caste of the builder.

This type of house resembles, down to points of detail, the stereotyped houses in rows which gave the cities of the Indus valley civilization their monotonous aspect. The excavations carried out by Sir John Marshall at Taxila brought to light the remains of an Aryan city built at a later date, named Sirkap. In his report Marshall wrote that the city of Sirkap was composed of several huge blocks, separated from one another by narrow streets. Although the ground-plans of the houses varied greatly, they nevertheless adhered to the same underlying principle. The basic structural unit was invariably an open square surrounded by rooms; this unit was repeated two, three or four times, or even more frequently, according to the number of rooms required by the inhabitants.

The great impact which the climate of a country has upon the structure of dwelling-houses is evident from the fact that the Aryan invaders, after they had completely wiped out or absorbed the Indus valley civilization and had become urbanized themselves, apparently arrived at just the same kind of plan as that favoured by their predecessors. Very similar houses of several storeys, built around a small central court or 'atrium', are still found in India today.

Apart from the popular catushālā type of house, a prospective owner can choose between the following types: 'trishālā', 'dvishālā' and 'ekshālā'. As these names indicate (shālā means house), the trishālā type has three wings arranged in a U pattern; a dvishālā is a house with two wings set at right angles, and an ekshālā is a simple rectangular building.

If the builder is not satisfied with any of these basic types of house, because the front and rear doors cannot be located in the proper place, then he has to consult a catalogue in which all the permissible combinations are listed. Each of the 14,000 possibilities has a name of its own. If he decides on one of these variants, he must again ensure that no deviations occur from the closely defined model form. The canonical rules leave no room for any later modifications, particularly expansion.

Archaeological finds do not necessarily endorse the theory that the strict Hindu building rules were a direct legacy of the urban civilization of the Indus valley, but the same laws also seem to have governed the appearance of Harappā and Mohenjo-daro.

One particularly striking feature of these two cities is that after every natural catastrophe sustained during their thousand-year existence the houses were rebuilt with the walls in the same position as they had been before, stone by stone and brick by brick. But paradoxically it was precisely this very rigid adherence to tradition, this need to restore exactly what had existed previously, that led to a change in the appearance of the city: the outside walls of the houses in the Indus valley towns had a slight tendency to lean inwards, copying the earlier clay buildings. When the city was devastated by some catastrophe, the rubble was not removed, as it was thought simpler to rebuild it on the new higher level. Since the house walls sloped, in the course of time the streets became ever broader and the houses ever narrower. If the Aryans had not put an end to these cities, after another millennium or two the inhabitants would have been faced with the alternative of either turning their cities into a wasteland of streets or of breaking with tradition.

Plates

Mahaballipuram

63 The shore temple is one of the first stone temples in the south Indian dravida style. It was built half in the sea and half on land, in the 7th–8th century A.D., and was used for ceremonies in which water played a major part.

64–65 The so-called rathas (celestial chariots) are forerunners of the south Indian stone temple. They were models, hewn out of a granite ridge. Most of them have no interior, since the builders were primarily concerned with trying to achieve the most suitable external form.

66 One of the rathas, Bhīma-ratha, had a barrel roof such as is found in chaitya-halls.

67 The miniature temples on the roofs of the rathas depict portable wooden shrines.

68 The Dharmarāja-ratha, a square temple with a pyramid-shaped roof, was chosen from a variety of possible types of temple as the model for all those later built in the dravida style. A procession of miniature shrines borne by animals is shown moving around the centre of the temple, in three tiers.

69 The Dharmarāja-ratha is crowned by a dome over an octagon.

Elūrā

70 The Kailāsa temple, executed in the dravida style, is the largest monolithic sanctuary in India.

71 View of the Kailāsa temple from the east of the main tower (vimāna). In contrast to other sanctuaries, the Kailāsa temple is oriented toward the west.

72 Only once in the whole temple enclosure, on the roof of the vestibule, does one find the geometric form of the circle. In Hindu 'metageometry' the circle symbolizes the earth in its material aspect. The square vimāna, as an image of the celestial spheres, stands in contrast to the symbolic rendering of the terrestrial world.

73 Relief scenes, from the epics of the 'Rāmāyana' and 'Mahābhārata', on the walls of the lower storey.

Tanjore

74 The entrance towers of the Brihadeshvara temple, dating from the 11th century A.D., seen from the south-west.

75 The tower (vimāna) over the cella, seen from the south-west. At Tanjore it was executed in gigantic dimensions.

76 The Subrahmanya shrine, dating from the 17th century A.D., shows how the monumental style, an expression of the imperial idea, was beginning to dissolve in an exaggerated differentiation of the formal canon.

77 Details of the Subrahmanya temple.

78 The lower storeys of the temple tower, seen from the north.

79 The 'Hall of One Thousand Lingams' stands inside the enclosure walls, between the ambulatory halls and small shrines containing images.

Madurai

80–81 The gate-towers (gopuras) through which one enters this circular temple city in south India soar above its countless halls and corridors. They were built around a very small cella tower ('centre') and increase in size the further they are from it.

82 The extravagant detail of this row of pilasters shows the decline of the dravida style.

83 Two gopuras in the northern part of the city, seen from the South Gopura.

84 Only at a few places does daylight enter the dark vestibules leading to the sanctum.

85 A columnar hall by the pool used for ritual ablutions.

86 In the wooden ceilings of the storeys of the gopura openings were left free so that the supplies and temple treasure, which were stored there, could be moved more easily.

The Kailāsa temple at Elūrā
Ground-plans, section and elevation 1:1000

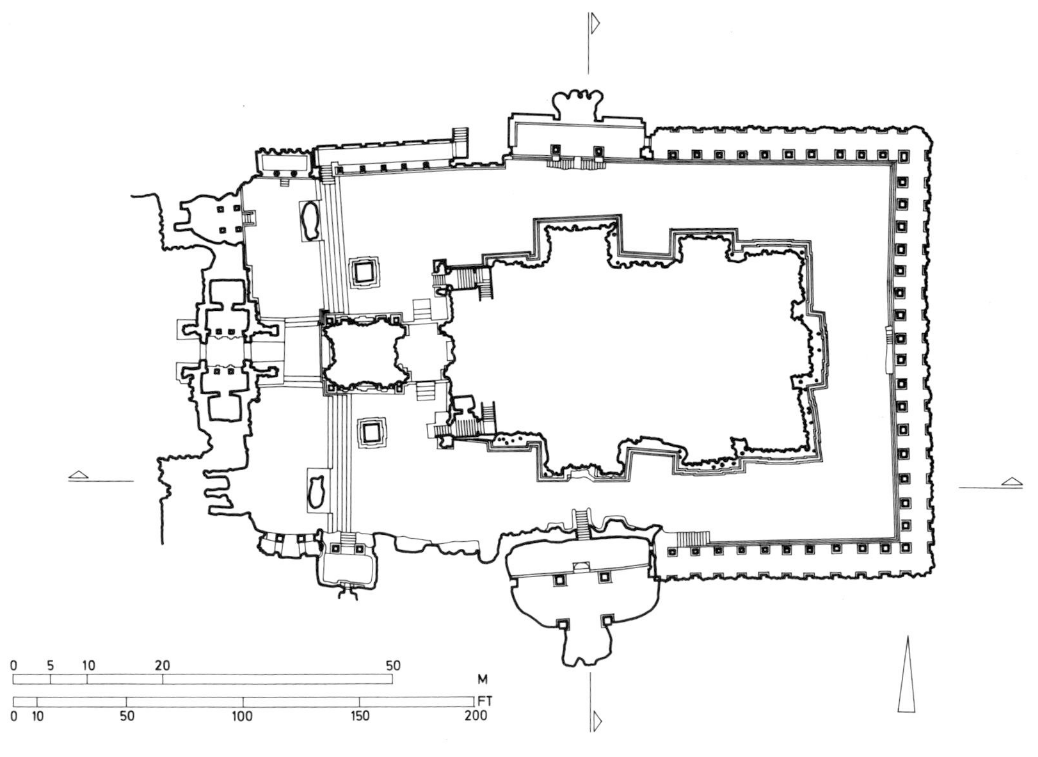

Monolithic column in the court of the temple 1:100

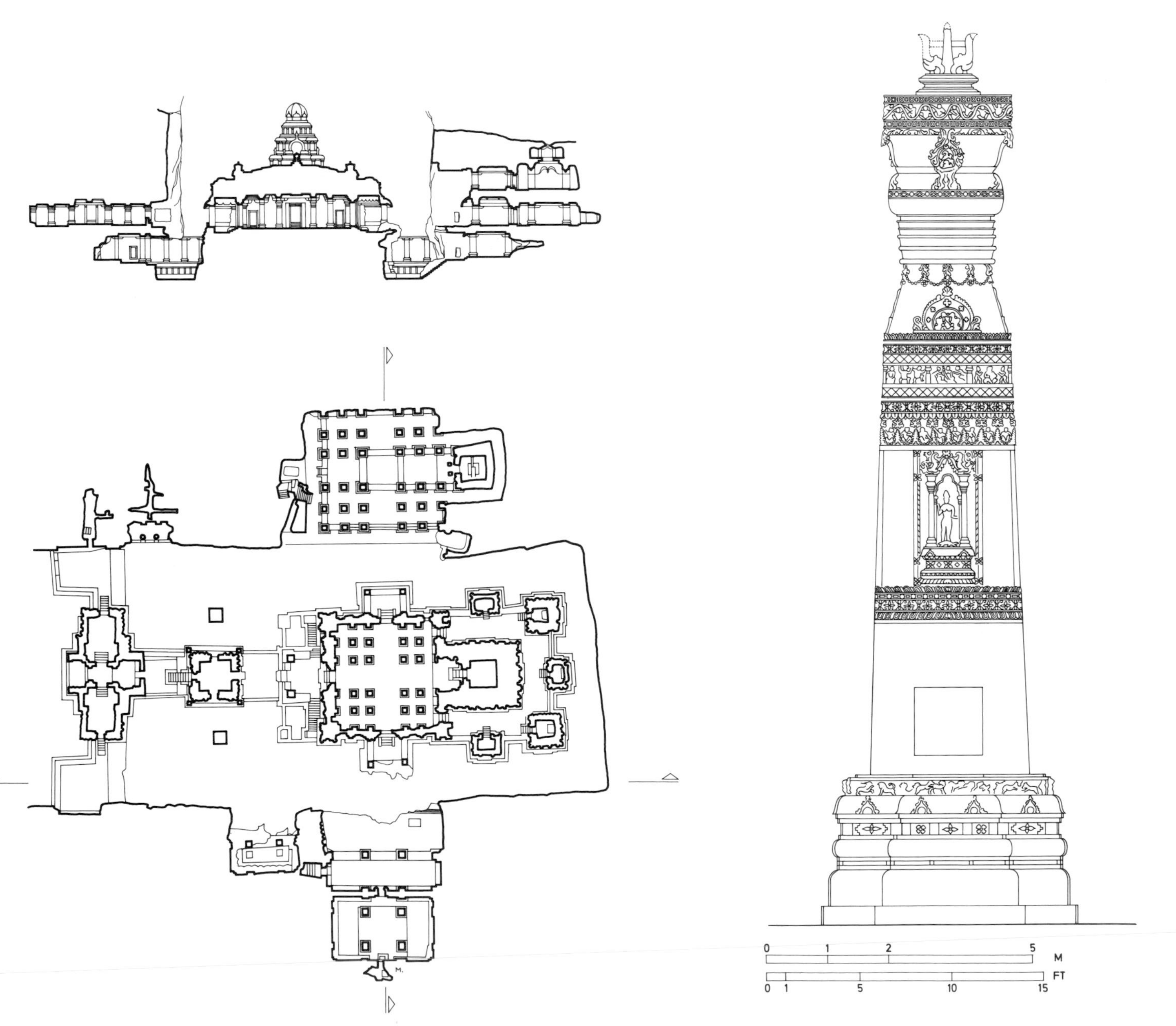

Notes

Mahaballipuram

It was not until the middle of the first millennium A.D. that the rulers of south India professed Hinduism. The Hindu period of Pallava and Chola architecture is introduced by the rathas of the seventh century A.D. One of these, the Dharmarāja-ratha, with its square ground-plan, became the model for the so-called dravida style of south India. The shore temple at Mahaballipuram is one of the first 'structive' temples to imitate this prototype.

Elūrā

In the neighbourhood of Ajantā are the rock-cut sanctuaries of Elūrā. As well as a Buddhist chaitya-hall, several Buddhist monasteries and some rock-cut Jain temples, there is a spacious Hindu sanctuary, the Kailāsa temple, which the local inhabitants call the 'ranga-mahal' (coloured palace). Since Krishna I, the donor of the Kailāsa temple, was unable to derive a Hindu type of temple from the architectural tradition of his own district, he copied the Pallava kings of the seventh century in summoning architects from the subject Chalukya kingdom. They developed further the ground-plan of the Virupaksha temple at Pattadkal and designed a monolithic sanctuary with several storeys, flights of steps, verandahs, halls and bridges. Just as much attention was paid to the treatment of the exterior as to the interior.

Tanjore

The Chola dynasty amalgamated the kingdoms of south India into a powerful empire. All the conquered areas, including even the island of Ceylon, had to pay tribute not only to the sovereign but also to the Brideshvara temple at Tanjore, a newly erected (11th-century) monument dedicated to one of the king's victories. This Shivaite sanctuary was built in the relatively short span of six years by Rājarāja the Great. The granite used in its construction seems to have been quarried at Mammalai, some thirty miles away. The Chola style reflects the prosperity and self-confidence of a dynasty which – not unlike the Romans in the Mediterranean – once it had consolidated its power gathered together all the artistic tendencies in south India and blended them into a monumental architectural style. According to certain inscriptions on the bases of temples, after all his triumphant successes the king had only one desire: that 'the temple should lack nothing'. The cities of his empire were obliged to supply cows and buffaloes from which fat was obtained for the temple lamps; they had to provide camphor, cardamon oil and other spices for the water used to wash the divine image; they had to supply goldsmiths, scribes, washermen, joiners, musicians, overseers and astronomers. Besides this the temples of the empire were compelled to send 212 attendants and their most beautiful dancing girls. For the 400 dancing girls who came to Tanjore a separate district of the town was built, close to the sacred compound.

Madurai

The foundation of this temple city is already mentioned in the 'Pūranas' (legends from prehistoric times). In the virgin forest a certain Indian found a Shiva lingam of divine origin. He built a cella and a temple around a stone phallus. A merchant by the name of Dhananjayan spoke of this to the south Indian king Kulasekhara Pandyan (1600 B.C.). He had the forest cleared and around the sanctuary built the city of Madurai. It was, however, not until the period between the twelfth and sixteenth century A.D. that the temple city was enlarged to its present form.

In the mid-twentieth century this dilapidated complex was renovated. The expense involved amounted to two and a half million rupees (about a quarter of a million dollars). A referendum was held, and as a result it was decided to paint the gopuras (gate-towers) in the original bright colours mentioned in inscriptions.

The two cellas of the interior of the temple enclosure are dedicated to the god Shiva, under the name of Sundareshvara, and to the goddess Meenakshi, an incarnation of Shiva's consort Pārvatī, whom he married at Madurai. The wedding-day of Sundareshvara and Meenakshi is still celebrated annually, and is the greatest of the festivals held in this temple city.

The Brihadeshvara temple at Tanjore
Ground-plan 1:1000 and vertical section of the cella structure (without the tower) 1:200

A Sanctuary (garbha)
B Artha-mandapa
C Mahā-mandapa
D Nandi-mandapa
E Gopura
F Shrine of Subrahmanya

0 1 5 10 M
0 1 5 10 20 30 FT

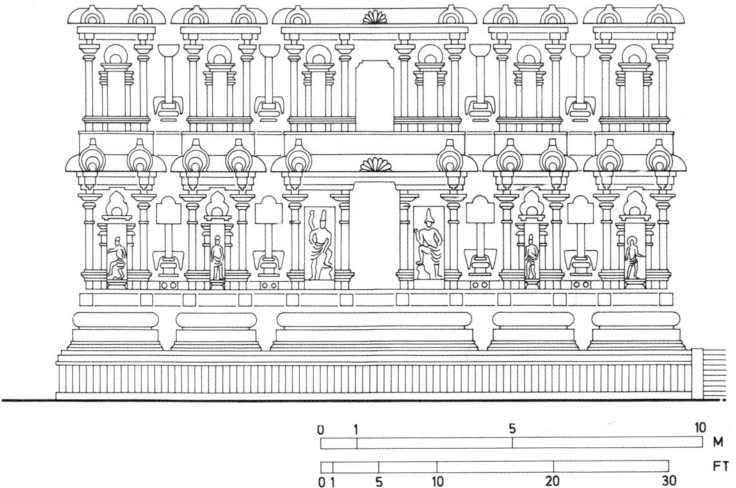

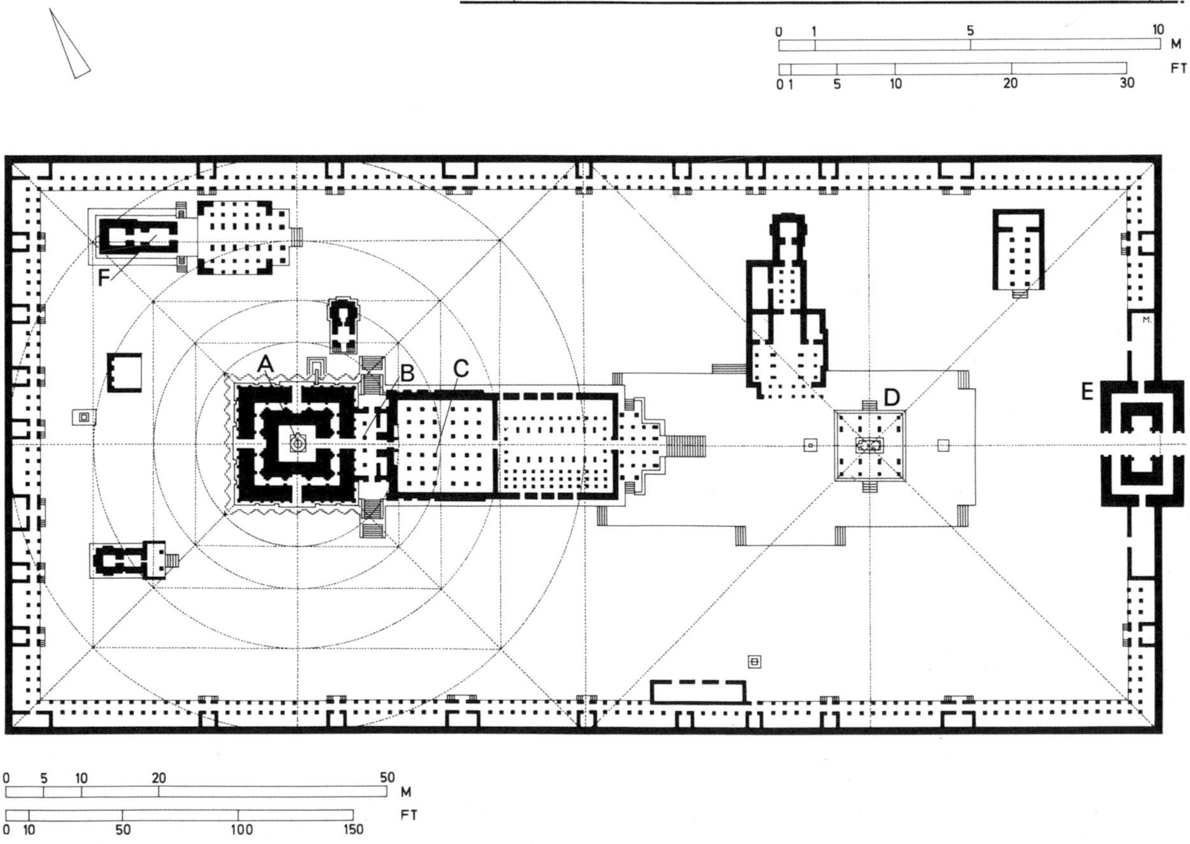

A
B
C
D
E
F
0 5 10 20 50 M
0 10 50 100 150 FT

The temple city of Madurai
Plan 1:3000

A Shrine of Sundareshvara
B Shrine of Meenakshi
C Temple pond
D South Gopura
E Hall of One Thousand Pillars

Section through the South Gopura 1:500

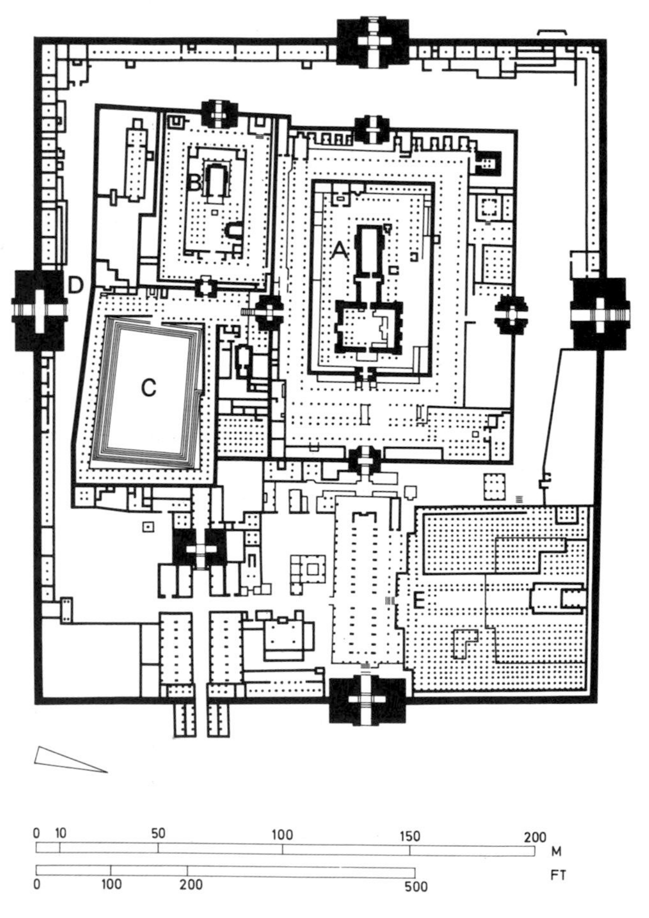

0 10 50 100 150 200 M
0 100 200 500 FT

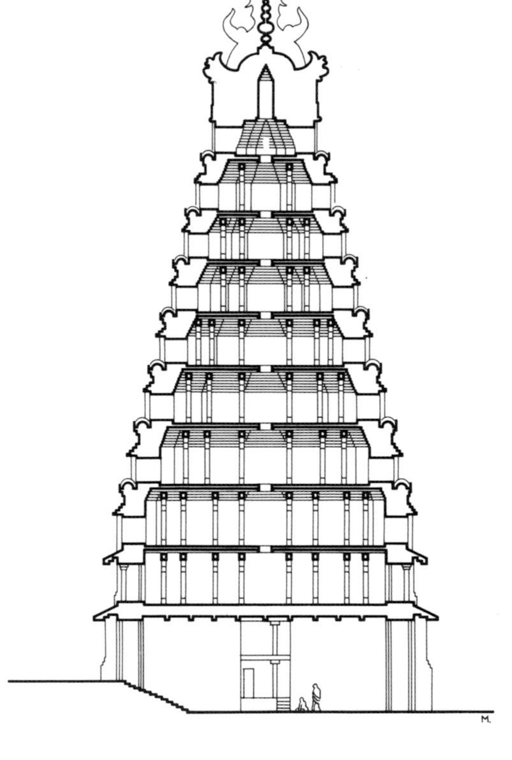

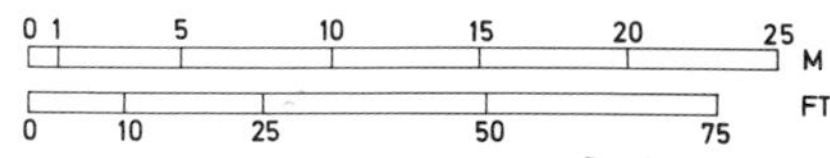

3. Buddhist Monuments: Stūpas and Chaitya-Halls

Stūpas (burial and relic mounds)

In reconstructing the earliest architectural forms of the Indian sub-continent, we are primarily dependent upon conclusions drawn 'a posteriori' from later buildings in stone. There were undoubtedly artistic wooden monuments in the north Indian cities prior to the middle of the first millennium B.C., but unfortunately no trace of them has as yet come to light.

We do, however, have a Megalithic culture in southern and central India dating from the middle of the second millennium B.C., the remains of which give some valuable indications about likely parallel developments in north India. As with the Megalithic cultures of the Mediterranean and northern Europe in the second millennium B.C., a highly developed cult of the dead led to the construction of extensive areas of dolmens, rows of stones and finally to the erection of stone cist-graves above and below the earth's surface. This form of grave, reserved mainly for tribal chieftains and heroes, as a rule consisted of four staggered stone slabs which formed the chamber walls, several stone slabs of the same size which served as the foundation and floor, and a huge cap-stone. Occasionally the cap-stone had a curved surface. Over the grave at Brahmāgiri (cf. p. 90) there was only a flat stone slab. All around the burial chamber rubble of flat stones was heaped up in a circle, forming the base and defining the outer limits of the earth mound which covered the entire structure.

A similar monumental burial mound was also common in north India during the lifetime of the Buddha. The Enlightened One himself instructed his disciples to commemorate great kings and sages by erecting at cross-roads so-called stūpas, mounds of earth enclosing a relic. From Buddhist texts we can see how widely they were disseminated and how popular they were. We are told that after the death of the Buddha eight of the mightiest princes fought among themselves for the ashes and bones of his mortal body. Each of them wanted to erect a huge stūpa above these relics.

In the second century B.C. the stūpa had the following form. A square, or alternatively circular, base, called 'medhi', was made of baked brick, set in clay. Upon this platform the hemispherical 'anda' (egg) was erected, one layer after another. The heaped-up earth over Megalithic graves had an outline or contour roughly in the shape of a hyperbola. This led to the idea of giving the reliquary the symbolic abstract form of a sphere or hemisphere. Since the diameter of the anda was in most cases less than that of the medhi, there was room for a raised path for processions (pradakshinā-patha). The flights of steps leading up to this path and the terrace were furnished with a wooden railing ('vedikā'), embedded in the brick. From the crown of the anda there rose a wooden mast, which often ran right through the stūpa from top to bottom. It bore the ancient oriental royal emblem of the umbrella ('chattravalī'). Mast and umbrella were surrounded by a square wooden railing, which in its structure resembled that on the platform.

This stone cist-grave from Brahmāgiri already anticipates important elements of stūpa symbolism

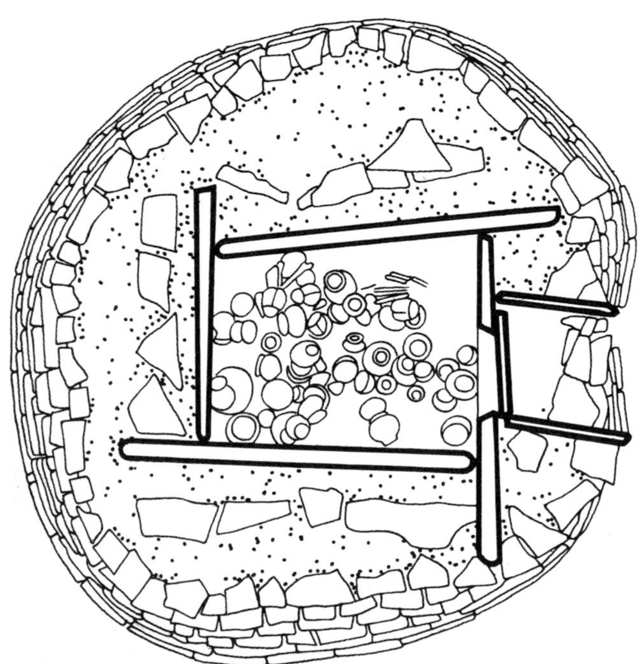

Where in the stūpa was the most important object, the reliquary, located? In early stūpas it was no doubt invariably in the centre of the sphere, i.e. on the platform. This situation was suggested by earlier Megalithic tombs, which had the burial chamber in the middle, and of greater importance was the fact that the whole shape of the stūpa would be meaningless unless the earth mound and brick casing were built around this central point. Notwithstanding considerations of this kind the relic was, however, often placed in a cubic receptacle ('harmikā') on the crown of the dome. A shift of the ritual centre only became possible after the stūpa had lost its original significance as a burial mound, during the reign of Ashoka, and had become an interminably repeated symbol of the teaching and cosmology of the Buddha. The cubic chamber of a Megalithic tomb, which incidentally may also be interpreted as a prototype of the Hindu cella, was replaced in the stūpa by the reliquary, which was moved from the centre of the anda to its summit; the rounded form of the anda became the image of the infinite cosmos. The Aryan symbol of the axis of the universe, the tree in the middle of the village under which the elders took counsel, re-appears in the stūpa as a vertical wooden axis.

The increased height of these monuments was at all times regarded also as an analogy between man and the cosmos, such as we have already learnt from the vāstu-purusha mandala of a Hindu temple. In the stūpa the medhi is the abdomen, the anda is the upper part of the body, and the honorary umbrella surrounded by the railing, or the urn containing the relic, is the head. Thus it is also understandable that eyes should have been painted on the harmikā of a stūpa at Kātmāndū, the core of which dates from as early as Ashoka's reign.

Sāñchī

Bimbisāra, king of Magadha and contemporary of the Buddha, built near his capital a monastery in which the Enlightened One and his disciples could take shelter during the monsoon season. In the choice of a suitable location the king took into account that this

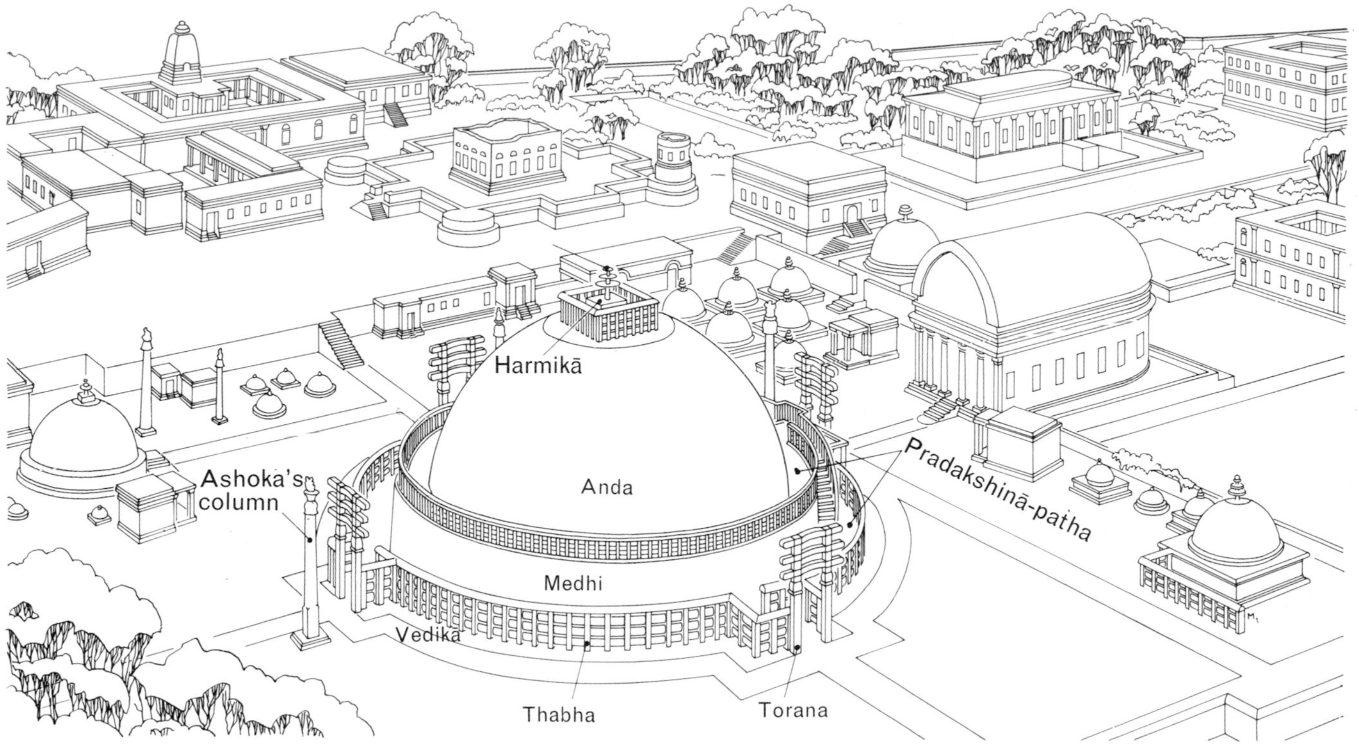

Reconstruction of the monastery at Sāñchī. In the foreground is the Great Stūpa

monastery 'must not be too far from the city but also not too close to it, within easy reach of all the people, and yet during the day not too crowded and at night not too noisy and dangerous, free from the odours of the populace, and finally a place concealed from the general view and well suited for a secluded life.'

Proximity to a city was of importance for Buddhist monasteries as the monks were obliged to go begging for half of every day. But the religious duties with which the other half of their days was filled made it seem inapposite to site a monastery within the confines of a noisy town. For this reason large Buddhist monastic communities sought a situation a few miles outside a city or on a busy trade route. This tradition accounts for the location of, for example, the monastery at Sārnāth, not far from Kashi (the present-day Benares) and of the equally well-known monastic complex at Taxila. The sanctuary at Sāñchī owed its existence and prosperity to the nearby trading centre of Vidisha, which was situated at the confluence of two rivers and developed into a significant meeting-point of two caravan routes, one running from north to south and the other from east to west.

The first small monastery on the mountain ridge at Sāñchī, which was maintained by the merchants of Vidisha, was on one occasion visited by Ashoka. At that time the future emperor was still crown prince and viceroy. He was travelling from Pātaliputra to his residence at Ujjain, and at Vidisha married the daughter of a distinguished banker.

After the collapse of the Maurya dynasty Vidisha

became the royal residence of the Shungas, and one of the most powerful cities in central India. Under Gupta rule it declined, and as a result the monastery at Sāñchī was deprived of the economic basis of its existence. In the thirteenth century A.D., if not earlier, Sāñchī was abandoned by the last monks to live there.

It was not until 1818 that General Taylor discovered, under the dense foliage of the jungle, the monastery buildings, which were still in a good state of preservation. Among British art historians the news quickly spread that a pre-Christian Buddhist foundation had been discovered, and within a few years amateur archaeologists and treasure-seekers had destroyed what the jungle had conserved for more than half a millennium. It was not until 1900 or thereabouts that systematic restoration was begun of those parts that remained.

Ashoka summoned from Persia sculptors to erect pillars on which his edicts were to be inscribed. Free-standing columns were already known in India – the inspiration for such monumental memorial columns may have come from the wooden columns in front of Hindu temples – but their formal execution clearly points to prototypes from Persepolis. The manner in which they were worked was likewise of alien origin: the surface of the hard sandstone from Chūnar was polished until it was as smooth as a mirror. The process employed to create such a splendid effect, which was characteristic of all columns and caves of the Maurya period, is unknown. The granite from which the Lomas Rishi and Sudāma caves were hewn is well suited for polishing, whereas this is to a much lesser extent the case with the sandstone from which these columns were carved.

In the sanctuary at Sāñchī are the remains of one of Ashoka's columns. This corroborates the story, hitherto in doubt, that Ashoka stopped here on his way to Ujjain. In the same archaeological stratum in which the base of the column was found, are the beginnings of a brick stūpa, likewise donated by Ashoka. In order to obtain a horizontal surface for this monument, the undulating ridges in the ground were carefully levelled. The cylindrical base and the circular structure were executed on a massive scale, in baked brick set in clay; the diameter measured 20 metres. Above the crown of the anda rose a multi-tiered honorary umbrella in sandstone, worked and polished in the same way as the columns. The same stone from Chūnar was used as was chosen for an honorary umbrella of the stūpa at Sārnāth. At Sārnāth a further step was taken in the use of this popular material: the balustrade around the umbrella was a true monolithic copy of the usual wooden structure.

The railing (vedikā) which surrounds the relic urn or cosmic tree and the umbrella is suggestive of an ancient Aryan motif. The Aryans were fond of fencing in sacred trees, sacrificial places and the like even though this was not necessary for practical reasons. Thus a town or village would not only be surrounded by a defensive wall but also by a railing, as a realization of a vāstu-purusha mandala. This originally consisted of closely packed thick posts, joined to one another by interlaced bamboo cross-bars. It could be of any height, and afforded ample protection against nocturnal predatory animals, lured close to the open hearths of the tribesmen. From this fence in its original form there evolved the high palisades of the eighth to sixth centuries B.C. which were used to protect cities.

The ancient Vedic railing around the village gave rise, not only to palisades suitable for military purposes, but also to a lighter transparent version, used primarily to mark the limits of a temple area. Through the wooden uprights ('thabha') were fitted either horizontal bamboo rods or, in the case of taller and more massive examples, levelled-off tree-trunks with lenticular cross-section. In cross-section these have the form alternately of a square or an octagon: for example, a square at the lowest point, an octagon in the middle, and another square at the end of the shaft.

The first treasure-seekers and private scholars who did such great damage to the so-called 'Great Stūpa of Sāñchī' were disappointed when they did not find a shrine containing relics either in the centre of the hemispherical dome or in its base. Presumably this shrine, whether it was placed inside or upon the crown of the dome, had previously fallen into the hands of Hindus who had been incited to destroy all Buddhist monasteries during the wave of persecution of Buddhists under the first Shunga king, Pushyamitra.

The succeeding Shunga kings lent their support to Buddhism. Under their patronage, in about 150 B.C. the original brick stūpa, which had been badly damaged, was expanded to double its former diameter and was encased in ashlar masonry, which has been preserved to the present day. A new hemispherical dome was gradually built up, one course after another, and the spaces in between filled with rubble stones. Instead of the ancient wooden railings stone balustrades were now erected around the crown and around the terrace on the medhi. The new dimensions did not permit a monolithic execution modelled on Sārnāth. The builders therefore reverted to techniques derived from the working of wood. The uprights, including the ornamental medallions and the tenons which tie the uprights to an upper terminal beam, were recarved in stone. Like their prototypes, they were provided with lenticular cavities into which separate cross-beams were mortised; these were also reworked. Such a costly reconstruction may not seem to us to do justice to the material used; nevertheless in the context of what could be realized at this time the builders could hardly have produced a more stable construction of similar appearance. There is no discrepancy between the technique chosen and the material; such a discrepancy does exist between the form and the material, but then the form was sanctified by tradition and could not be changed.

The new stone stūpa, enlarged to a diameter of 36.6 metres, was given a third stone railing, at ground level, about 3 metres from the medhi. Thus the circumambulation of the stūpa at ground level, which had been customary for a long time, was integrated into the architecture. From the need to bring the lower railing into a proper relationship with the enlarged stūpa, the dimensions of the uprights and cross-bars were greatly exaggerated. The lower vedikā of the Great Stūpa measures 3.15 metres in height and is the largest of all the railings known; each 'lath' of the railing weighs several tons. From the number of uprights – there are precisely 120 of them – it can be inferred that rules of measurement govern all the architectural elements of Buddhist stūpas as well as those of Hindu temples.

The ends of the swastikas which constitute the approaches to the lower pradakshinā-patha symbolize the course of the sun. The custom of circumambulation was closely connected with ancient solar cults, as is shown by the fact that the procession always begins in the east and follows the course of the sun southwards and then westwards. The number of uprights is presumably related to the division of the zodiac into twelve parts and to the division of the sun's course from horizon to horizon into twelve hour-angles.

The Buddha had, in his own words, set in motion 'the wheel of doctrine'. The roundness of the wheel became the basic form in Buddhist 'metageometry'. The supreme goal of the Buddhist is to escape from the cycle of earthly suffering. As he sees it, all growth and decay is reflected in the circular form; to escape from the cycle means to be wafted away into the formless nirvāna.

The two flights of steps leading to the medhi on the south side of the Great Stūpa brought about an involuntary narrowing of the circumambulatory path at this point. For this reason the lower vedikā was made to deviate from the circular shape until it provided a sufficiently wide passage. This compromise necessitated another. In front of the old brick stūpa Ashoka's column had stood at a well-proportioned distance; now, after the enlargement of the stūpa, the column was closer to its base. The old stūpa was oriented exactly towards the cardinal points and the column stood exactly on the north-south axis. If the new ground-level vedikā, with its approaches, had been oriented in the same way, Ashoka's column would have stood some two metres in front of the entrance; and, if a swastika form were chosen for the ends of the vedikā, it would even stand in the centre of the entrance. A neat solution of the problem seemed impossible. It was therefore decided to turn the entire stūpa, together with the flights of steps and the lower entrances, in a clockwise direction by a certain degree. It seemed worth putting up with an error in the orientation in order to preserve the column. It would of course also have been possible to move just one of the entrances, namely the southern one. But this solution obviously seemed to the architects a violation of the firmly fixed image of the cosmos, and for this reason they rejected it.

Let us note that the entrances were originally planned and executed without the splendid gates ('toranas') and without the section of railing marked on our plan as (a). The bulge at the end of the swastika to the left of the approach meant that the procession could not move toward the stūpa along its axis, but had to approach the pradakshinā-patha tangentially and in a clockwise direction. If one wanted to leave the circumambulatory path, the approaches were inconvenient, since all four bulges of the railing merely led 'into' the path and not 'out of' it. We must therefore not only interpret their structure from the functional point of view but also see in it primarily those elements, derived from solar symbolism, that set the circle of the railing in motion. It is through them that the stūpa ground-plan appears to rotate, either as the Wheel of Doctrine, or as the course of the sun, or as the infinite cosmos, or as the rotation of the relic.

Access to the circumambulatory path of the Great Stūpa at Sāñchī, showing the two stages in its construction

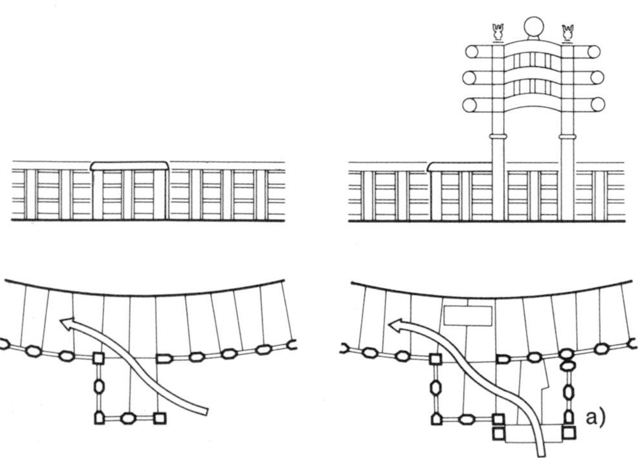

At the time of the Āndhras, who succeeded the Shungas, the entrances to the lower circumambulatory path were rebuilt. To the original opening in the railing a second one was added, but at an angle to it; simultaneously a splendid gate (torana) was built at the end of the swastika and a new piece of railing (a) added, so bringing out the entrance more clearly and closing it off. The principle of a tangential approach to the pradakshinā-patha was thus abandoned.

The entrance gates form a striking contrast to the body of the stūpa. Whereas the hemispherical dome of the stūpa is composed of crudely-hewn stone courses, the gates are covered with reliefs and are elaborately worked. In constructing the toranas the builders kept strictly to the wooden prototypes as they are depicted in the reliefs on the city gates. Each gate, supported by elephants, stands upon two rectangular pillars. Their three architraves and intermediate parts are crowned by a carving of the 'dharmacakra', 'the Wheel of the Law'. The uprights terminate in the 'triratna' symbol (three jewels), which represents the foundation of the doctrine, i.e. the Buddha, the law and the congregation.

When the attempt was made at Sāñchī to translate the form of the wooden city gate into stone on a monumental scale, a number of structural problems arose. Since most believers were illiterate, scenes from the Jātaka legends (stories about the early life of the Buddha as a Bodhisattva) were represented in a sequence of reliefs. The animal and human figures which fill the spaces between the architraves were occasionally given faces on both sides, since no agreement could be reached as to whether the sculptures were to face the processional path (and the relic) or the people who would look at the monument from outside. In many tales the urban environment plays a major part, and attempts therefore had to be made to represent buildings. Reliefs which had been treated two-dimensionally on every respect were now given three-dimensional depth by graduating the representations of buildings, i.e. by depicting them one behind the other and overlapping but without obtaining a genuine perspective.

It would appear reasonable to assume that the stūpa itself is not only an unsystematic stratification of stone but contains an interior pregnant with symbolism, corresponding to the symbolism of the exterior. But the stūpas of the Ashoka period disappoint us in this respect. They are still so closely linked to the burial-mound motif that cosmological concepts did not exert any influence upon their construction. It is a different matter in the case of the innumerable stūpas built during the second and third centuries A.D. at Nāgārjunakonda, a Buddhist centre in south India. Here, on the river Krishnā, Buddhist monks transformed several square miles of flat land into a landscape of glittering white stūpas. Four of them – only their lower courses are still extant – enclose a swastika built facing the cardinal points. All the other stūpas at Nāgārjunakonda are built on the plan of a wheel with spokes.

In the construction of these numerous votive stūpas, owing to a shortage of easily obtainable stone, building could be only in brick and earth. The stone stūpas of north India owe their stability to a filling of squared rubble stones, which could not of themselves shift or cause shrinkage. A massive stūpa in brick was ruled out on economic grounds, in view of the size and number of stūpas at Nāgārjunakonda. For this reason the builders resorted to the technique of dividing the interior of the hemispherical dome into chambers by means of vertical wall sections, arranged radially, and filling these chambers with loose earth and small stones.

The swastika mentioned above as a feature of the ground-plan of several stūpas was carried up in the wall sections to the inner surface of the dome. The same was true of the ground-plan based on the wheel.

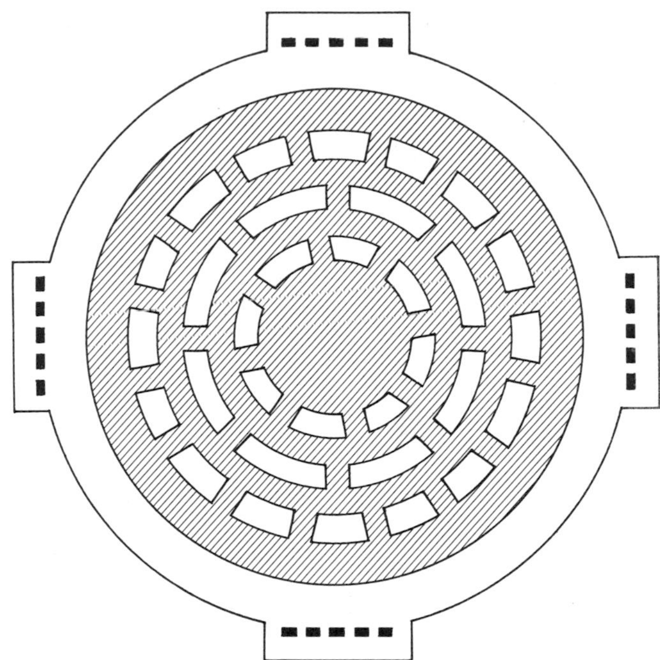

Ground-plan of the Great Stūpa at Nāgārjunakonda

The Great Stūpa at Nāgārjunakonda is of particular interest. The pillar in the centre is strikingly ponderous; three circular walls are placed concentrically around it, the outer one rising to form a dome over the entire construction. The partition walls in the inner zone correspond to a double number in the outer zone; the chambers of the middle zone are staggered in relation to those of the inner zone. This seems astonishing at first sight, since the inner and middle zones contain the same number of chambers, so that the inner partition walls could have been continued radially into the middle zone and finally into the double walls in the outer zone. Instead the following geometric relationship was preferred: of the sixteen outer chambers four point to the cardinal points; but in the middle zone it is not the chambers that do so, but four of the light partition walls between the chambers. The partition wall on the left (seen from the centre) of the eight partition walls between the chambers, which is oriented toward the major and minor cardinal points, is continued in the interior.

An accentuated centre and three graduated zones of rings: is this not reminiscent of the south Indian mandalas which we have discussed in Chapter II? Did the ancient Dravidian concept of a circular world find an echo in this stūpa – here in the south, far from the spiritual centres of Buddhism in north India? The similarity is staggering, if one leaves out of account the fact that Buddhist 'metageometry' is always based upon the circle, whereas Hindu 'metageometry' is mainly based upon the square. In considering this ground-plan we are tempted to see in it, not only the realms of gods, humans and demons, concentrated around Brahman, but also the special circular form of the vāstu-purusha mandala of north India, of which this ground-plan is reminiscent. At Nāgārjunakonda there are 16 outer panels; in the north Indian mandala there are as a rule 32 gods residing in the outer pādas. In each case the panels or chambers are oriented towards the cardinal points.

The most recent studies of stūpa geometry have led to the conclusion that the number of spokes was only determined by the size of the stūpa. Nevertheless both technical requirements and theological concepts undoubtedly led to the wheel- or swastika-shaped ground-plan. Most stūpas have four or eight spokes, a few of them six or ten, and three of the largest ones eight, twelve or sixteen, arranged in various zones.

Ground-plan and vertical section of the cave stūpa at Guntupalle

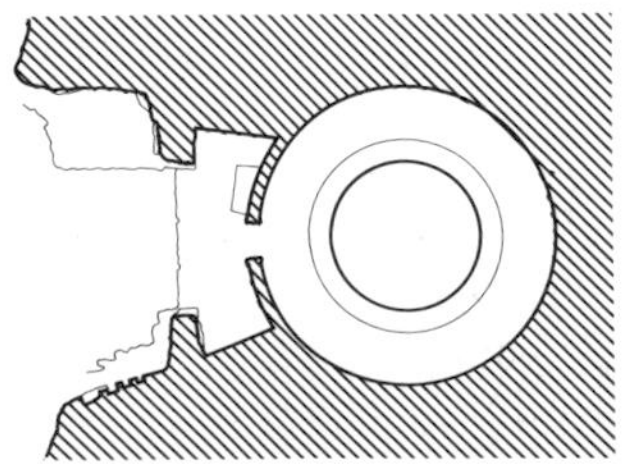

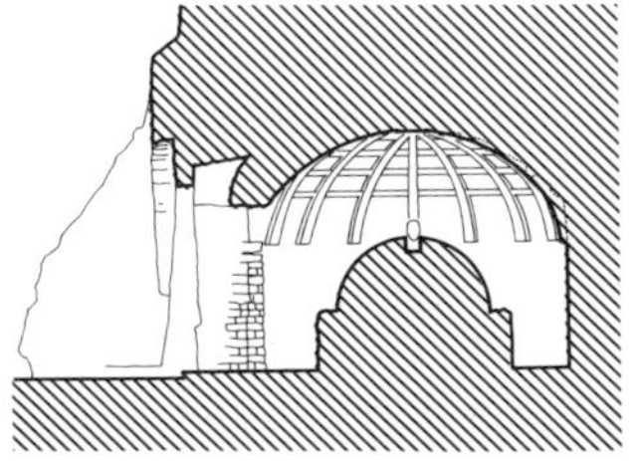

Chaitya-halls (prayer-halls)

The term 'chaitya' is derived from the Sanskrit word 'chita', the mound of ashes formed when a deceased person is cremated. Chaitya eventually came to mean the earth mound heaped up over the ashes of a saint or over a relic. Thus Buddhists occasionally referred to stūpas as chaityas. Stūpa (mound, head) is merely the architectural 'terminus technicus' for reliquary.

By chaitya-halls we mean those Buddhist monuments which enclose a stūpa. We do not know at which point in time Indians began to erect a protective building around the stūpa, since the first chaitya-halls were no doubt built of non-durable material, namely bamboo.

In considering what would be the proper enclosure for a stūpa, the architects chose as their model the existing form of a round clay or bamboo hut. This proved particularly appropriate to the purpose, since a circular pradakshinā-patha remained clear between the medhi and the wall of the house. The domed roof repeated the venerated form of the anda (egg), as though it were a second shell.

At Guntupalle (Madras state) archaeologists have discovered a round cave with a domed roof hewn out of the natural rock in imitation of a round wooden building. It contains a stūpa hewn out by the same method. The dome above the stūpa is copied from a basket-like wooden support.

According to Jouveau-Dubreuil, a cave near Tellichery (Kerala state) dates from the pre-Buddhist period: its hemispherical shape bears a striking resemblance to the Buddhist symbolic idiom, and it has in the centre a monolithic pillar, reaching from the floor of the cave to the roof. Is this merely a tradition-bound attempt to render in this form one of the early types of hut? (According to the sacred texts the first human dwellings were modelled upon a tree, with a

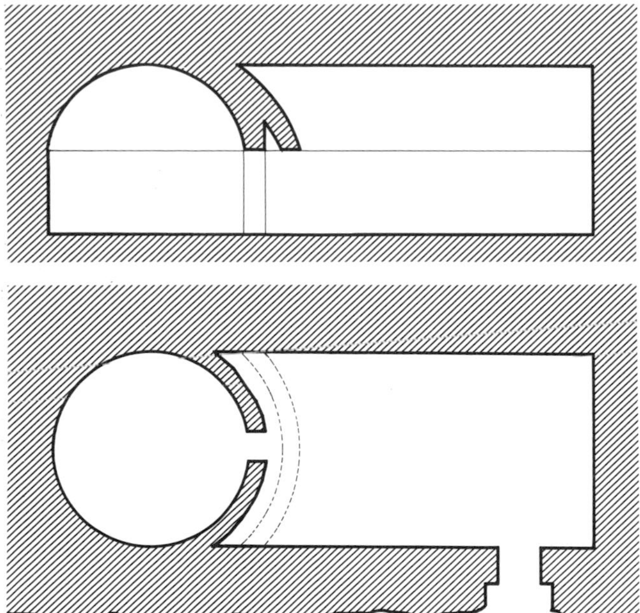

Section and ground-plan of Sudāma cave in the Barābar Hills, 3rd century B.C.

shaft in the centre from the apex of which a roof of leaves hung down to the ground on all sides.) Or is this the first representation of the cosmic axis and of the cosmos as a sphere, anticipating the view of the cosmos later encountered in Buddhism?

Besides the 'negative stūpa' at Tellichery and the stūpa-cave at Guntupalle we can mention a third type of domical roof as a prototype of the chaitya-hall. In the Barābar Hills (Bihar state) are two artificial caves, Sudāma and Lomas Rishi. Inscriptions record that the emperor Ashoka had these caves hewn out of the granite of this low ridge for a group of Ājīvikas (a sect which split off from the Jains). Access to the caves, which are rectangular in plan, is gained from one of the longitudinal sides. The ceiling is shaped like a barrel and the interior resembles a tunnel. At one end is an elaborately worked copy of a round house with a thatched domed roof. The modelling of the round house extends to such details as, for example, an overhanging roof (see section above) or the transformation of the circular ground-plan into a polygon, obtained by dressing the house with closely-packed rows of wooden planks. Both the domical and rectangular chambers are copied from contemporary dwelling-huts.

Several historians have posed the question why the entrances to the two caves (in the Sudāma cave it is an unpretentious trapezoid aperture; in the Lomas Rishi cave there is in addition the sculptural relief on the façade) were not placed in front but somewhere along the longitudinal wall. Does it not seem paradoxical to enter the cave by one of its longitudinal sides below a representation of a tympanum? More recent studies have clarified this point: the tympanum in relief must be a later addition. Detailed investigations into questions of style have shown that the relief does not originate from the reign of Ashoka but from that of a later Mauryan emperor. The new door frame was polished in the old technique, and the old trapezoid door fits into the new façade to form a logical and constructive entity. If we disregard this façade, then it is easier to understand why a door was inserted in the longitudinal wall. One recurrent theory is that the cave could not be sited vertically to the rock because the ridge was too narrow. However, this idea has several weaknesses. In the first place, the ridge is not narrow; secondly, if it had been, a different rock in the neighbouring mountains could have been chosen, or else the dimensions of the cave could have been adjusted to those of this particular rock. Thus the decisive reason for this mode of execution seems to have been that lateral entrances were quite common in ordinary dwellings.

Although the two caves were not hewn out of the rock by, or for, Buddhists, the very fact that they combined rectangular and circular chambers was to prove a significant landmark in the development of Buddhist architecture. Presumably the Ājīvika monks wanted to separate the cult chamber from the general living accommodation; the Buddhists employed the same sequence of rooms, since they needed, in addition to the stūpa area, an assembly hall for the communal public confession and for other occasions.

Both types of chamber, however, are treated as a single whole, which has one side terminating in a rectangle and the other in a rounded form. Above the rectangle is the barrel-vault, which was originally of bamboo, then of wood, and finally of stone; above the rounded apse is a quadrant. The high barrel-vaulting requires a lateral support, as does the nave of a Christian basilica. Thus low aisles were added, also arranged around the apse. The colonnades and barrel-vaulting of the nave are as a rule separated by a length of wall; but about the construction of this wall little is known.

During the second century B.C., at the time when in central India Ashoka's stūpa at Sāñchī was encased in stone, and the first stone stūpas were being erected, some monastic communities on the west coast began not only to build monasteries and prayer- or chaitya-halls of bamboo, wood and brick but also to hew them out of the sheer rock faces of the western Ghats.

Vertical sections of the brick-built chaitya-hall at Chezarla (false vault)

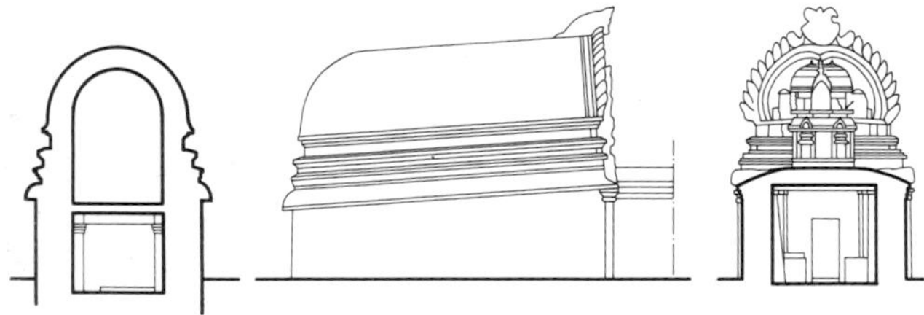

Ground-plan of Buddhist temple no. 18 at Sāñchī

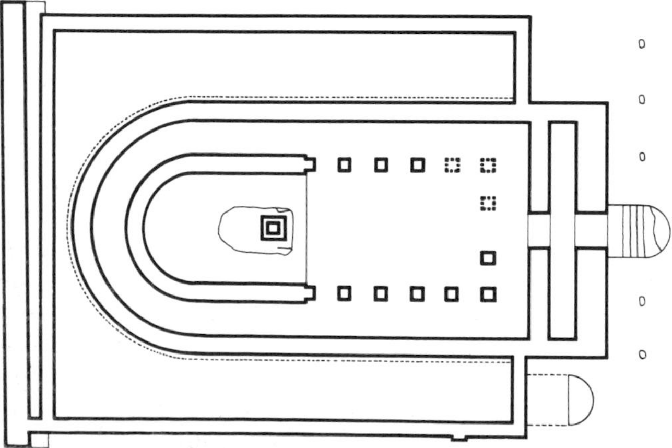

The combination of dome and barrel-vault had developed in wooden buildings of the third century B.C., i.e. in Ashoka's lifetime. The free-standing chaitya-halls were later constructed of brick as well as of wood. The earliest specimen to have survived is the Kapoteshvara temple at Chezarla, a Buddhist brick structure dating from the fourth century A.D. which was subsequently transformed into a Hindu temple. Spatial problems are solved in a similar way at Aihole (Durgā temple, Hindu) and at Sāñchī (temple no. 18, Buddhist), which likewise date from the Gupta period. In both cases the ground-plan shows a different treatment of the rectangular area and the apse. The colonnades in the assembly hall were not continued along the rounding of the apse but were replaced by a massive wall.

What sort of shape was given to the apse of the rock-cut chaitya-halls of the western Ghats? The earliest example, the cave at Bhājā, which was carved during the first decades of the second century B.C., provides clear evidence of the development from wood architecture in the inward slope of its octagonal columns. These are faithful copies of tree-trunks hewn octagonally and rammed into the soil at a slant to serve as fixed supports; the slant reduced the danger that the outward thrust of the vault could cause the building to collapse. A massive execution of the apse was not necessary in the wooden model, since all the fixed supports acted together to prevent any distortion of the building. For this reason in Bhājā the colonnades are continued unbroken in the apse.

Also the exterior walls of the aisles slope inwards, since they bear the weight of the walls over the colonnades as well as the thrust of quarters of the barrel-vaulting of the aisles. There is no architrave, such as one would expect above the dense colonnades in the

Cross-section of the monolithic chaitya-hall at Bhājā, 2nd century B.C.

nave, in order to distribute the weight of the walls equally. Presumably in the wooden prototype the entire wall, consisting of horizontal wooden beams, had the effect of a supporting structure. The ribs or wooden arches are dovetailed into the wall. By prolonging them vertically in the wall it was possible for the arch to be dowelled twice, thereby preventing the ribs from toppling over, especially while building was in progress. The kind of roofing employed can be seen from the façade. Over the horizontal beams resting on rafters was a thick layer of thatch.

Only with some hesitation did Buddhist architects dare to employ this new material, stone. All Hīnayāna chaitya-halls – these differ stylistically from Mahāyāna ones in that they do not represent the Buddha in any anthropomorphic form – are distinguished by the fact that the rock-cut parts are supplemented by wooden ones. The vault often rests upon the rock and does not have any wooden support, whereas the filling of the horseshoe-shaped window ('kudu') is always worked in wood.

By the time chaitya-halls began to be carved out of the vertical faces of rocky cliffs on the west coast, the stūpa had already lost its original meaning and use, and had become merely symbolic. To an increasing extent the anda became a visible sphere. At Bhājā this effect was obtained by adding to the hemispherical dome the uppermost section of the lower half of the sphere. The medhi shrank and finally the upper processional path was omitted completely. The reliquary came to form a single entity with its surrounding railing, and as a kind of altar took on some traditional Vedic formal elements.

The advantages of a rock-cut chaitya-hall were not confined to its durability. Esoteric reasons also account for the preference given to rock-hewn monuments in which the cult object, in its meaning as cosmic egg, could be represented directly in the 'primeval matter', stone, in the dark depths of a subterranean chamber, without the substance of the anda having to be transported or reconstructed by human hand.

It appears that as early as the second century B.C. the traditional forms of building fell into neglect and were superseded by rock-cut monuments. For no chaitya-halls are known which copy a fairly late phase of genuine wooden architecture. The process of stylistic development towards an ever-increasing profusion of forms takes place in stone, although wood continued to be used for barrel-vaulting and for horseshoe-shaped windows until late works of the Hīnayāna phase.

The chaitya-hall at Kondane, too, possessed a façade worked in wood. But in stone we have here a particularly detailed representation of the urban façades which in wooden prototypes extended on either side of the hall. All the details, including the dowelling, were rendered as though the level of technical development that had been achieved was to be put on record for all ages to come. In most early halls the architects concentrated on elaboration of the interior; the transition from the interior to the exterior of the building was only hinted at. Kondane is one of the exceptions, where the sequence of façades

Attempted reconstruction of a wooden chaitya-hall, after the monolithic façade of Kondane

was emphasized as strongly as the interior. From the reconstruction (see above) it can be seen that wood, not brick, let alone stone, was the chief material used in the prototypes of this rock-cut monument. Upper storeys projecting far out, overhanging 'roll cornices' and multi-tiered galleries can only be executed by delicate work in wood.

The archaeologists' disappointment at not being able to find the slightest trace of such a wooden basilica on the Indian sub-continent has recently led to the theory that the prototypes should be sought outside India. In Greece and Palestine rectangular halls with an apse were known at this time, but so long as the prototypes in question cannot be authenticated in lands adjacent to India, we shall adhere to the assumption that the chaitya-hall developed on Indian soil; this hypothesis is strengthened by the existence of vast numbers of renderings in relief of barrel-vaulted houses.

Several years after the monastery at Bhājā was founded work began on the monastic settlement of Ajantā, in the gorge of the Waghora river about 400 kilometres from the modern city of Bombay. Ajantā was to be enlarged on many occasions over the centuries. Today it enjoys world-wide fame chiefly on account of its wall-paintings, dating from the fifth century A.D. At one spot, where the Waghora cascades over a high waterfall into a deep chasm and then describes a wide curve, there are rows of large but unpretentious rock-cut halls, small chapels with lavish decoration, spectacular multi-storeyed rock-cut monasteries, the inconspicuous dwellings of individual ascetics. All are hewn out of the cliffs which line the curved bank of the river. From each prayer-hall and from the verandah of each monastery one can glimpse the sequence of communal buildings, laid out on various levels around this semicircular area. It is tempting to conceive of this veritable open-air museum, with its harmonious layout, as having been planned as a single unit. But the fact is that only a few Hīnayāna monasteries ('vihāras') and two chaitya-halls date from the period between the second century B.C. and the second century A.D., whereas the remaining caves were added in the Mahāyāna style four hundred years later.

Landslides then blocked all access to these caves. In 1817 a company of British troops on manoeuvre hit upon some gates that were visible amidst the scree, and efforts were made to unearth other entrances. Up to the present time 30 caves have been discovered. All were accessible from the floor of the valley by means of a narrow flight of steps in the rock. During the rainy season, for which the monasteries were chiefly

Cave monasteries of Ajantā: site plan

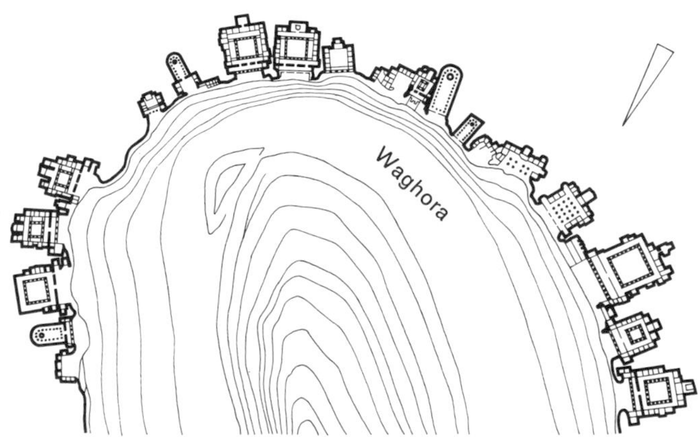

designed, the waters of the river rose and boats had to be used to reach one flight of steps from another. Only a few chaitya-halls and vihāras are interconnected. The path which leads along the cliff-face, from which most of the caves are now accessible, was only made during the last century.

The two Hīnayāna prayer-halls at Ajantā bear a resemblance to those at Bhājā. The only new features were that in one of them the entire façade was left in stone, and that many of the details were executed on the adjoining rock surface, with wooden lattice windows added here and there; furthermore, the columns in the interior do not slope so much and the anda is already close to the shape of an egg.

The culminating achievement of Hīnayāna architecture is Kārlī (see plan, p. 41). According to one inscription a certain 'Seth Bhutapala from the city of Vaijayanti' was the donor of 'this most unusual rock-cut monument in India'. He was assisted by a pharmacist, who bore the cost of the doors, by the preacher Satimita, who paid for one column with a reliquary built into it, by two mendicant monks, who raised the money for two other columns, and lastly by an ascetic, who points out in his inscription that a gift of this kind is 'exceedingly meritorious'. Let us not forget the Greeks, who paid for several columns, and another layman, who raised the money for a lion column flanking the main entrance. The donors were not exaggerating when they spoke of 'the most unusual rock-cut monument in India'. The cave at Kārlī is by far the largest in the Hīnayāna series; even during the Mahāyāna period, characterized by monumental style and great splendour, no attempt was made to emulate an undertaking conceived on such a gigantic scale as this.

The architects, or rather sculptors, of the preceding chaitya-halls could be reproached for adhering too slavishly to wooden prototypes. These limitations are cast off at Kārlī. The interior is such that it could neither have been conceived in wood nor executed in hewn stone. Rock-cut architecture has here achieved a unique and specifically monolithic chamber. Wood is used only where it greatly simplifies the builders' task or seems advisable for economic or structural reasons.

The nave is longer than in other caves. (The ratio of width to length is as follows: Bhājā 1:2.5; Ajantā 1:2.7; Kārlī 1:3.0.) The aisle not only runs round the apse but also forms a passage on the entrance side, separated from the nave by its own colonnade. Thus a step has been taken here which European architects only hit upon several centuries later, in the basilica of S. Sebastian in Rome.

In chaitya-halls built of brick or stone the different structure of the transition from nave to apse – in one case a colonnade, in the other masonry – was ascribed to the requirements of statics. The same explanation holds good for the first rock-cut halls, which had a uniform colonnade around the nave and the apse. However, the later Hīnayāna halls (Nāsik, Junnar and Kārlī) surprise us by having columns of different shape in the rounded and in the rectangular chamber. The columns surrounding the stūpa have the ancient simple form of unadorned wooden uprights. But the nave is lined by imitations of those 'stambhas' which were erected in front of the gates of a stūpa or a Hindu temple as early as Ashoka's reign.

It was in conformity with the Indian (Hindu as well as Buddhist) symbolic interpretation of the cosmos that the two animal sculptures which, at Persepolis, form part of the capital and support the beams should be replaced by the four guardians of the cardinal points. But as soon as multiple columns were needed for the interior this symbolic content had to be abandoned. The architect at Kārlī replaced the four animals of the Ashoka columns with mounted pairs of lovers. He had as yet no desire to abandon the animal motif completely, but allowed it to be dominated by renderings of mundane scenes. Now it will be clear why the nave and apse had to be fashioned in a different way. The rectangular area was the place where the faithful congregated. Here a profusion of forms and a joy in this-worldly things could develop freely. The rounded form of the apse, on the other hand, is centred solely upon the sacred form of the anda, and its transcendental connotations rule out any decoration.

From the circular shape of the burial mound and from the Wheel of the Law, frequently quoted by the Buddha, there developed in Buddhism a geometry of symbols which in part stands in contrast to that of Hinduism. The Hindu image of the cosmos originated in the Vedic period: in the beginning of time the world was a circular, unaligned manifestation, which was subjected by Brahmā to the cosmic principle of order by squaring the circle. In Buddhist architecture the circle merely symbolizes the supreme order, and we rarely encounter the square. At Nāgārjunakonda it determines the contour of the medhi, and at Kārlī the grid plan of the façade.

At Kārlī the themes of the exterior and the interior are only loosely linked. Neither the rendering of a wooden support within the horseshoe-shaped window nor the lathes of the roof, visible from outside, are continued logically in the forms of the barrel-vaulting. The teak arches of the roofing start a few centimetres above the colonnade, and there is no wall surface which could interrupt the flowing line of the arch. In defiance of all wooden prototypes the lowest points of the wooden ribs, which are 80 centimetres deep and 25 centimetres wide, seem to hover over the heads of the pairs of lovers. The impression of unreality is enhanced still further by a little artifice: the lowest points of the arches curve outward slightly.

The close alignment of the ribs conceals the smooth rock face above. This, aided by the exceptional height of the chamber and the use of different material for the colonnade and for the vaulting, produces the effect that, on entering, one would not imagine oneself to be standing in a rock-cut cave at all, but rather in the open air, in a colonnaded court which opens up toward the stūpa. The narrow intercolumnation and the close alignment of the arches also enhance this effect of depth. Only the reliquary with the honorary umbrella rises above the colonnades.

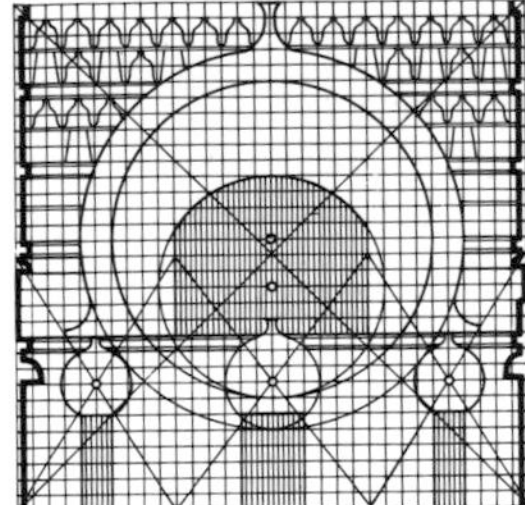

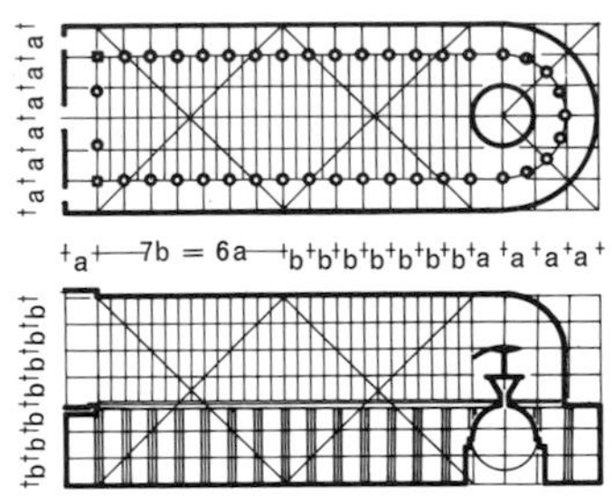

Left: canon of proportions of the façade of Kārlī, based on a grid with 32 × 32 panels
Right: ground-plan and vertical section of the chaitya-hall at Kārlī, showing the proportions

Every spatial element and every detail has been worked by the architect into a homogeneous vision of the whole chamber. It is hardly imaginable that this could have been possible without accurate planning, in three separate drafts. In this classical stage of rock-cut architecture it is also to be expected that the clear architectonic concept of the monument should be reflected in equally clear geometric relationships both in the ground-plan and in the vertical section. These expectations are not deceived: the basic measurement is provided by the stūpa. If one doubles its radius, one gets the axis of the colonnade; if one triples it, one obtains the width of the aisles, the inner width of the entire monument, and also its height. The ground-plan thus consists of six lengths, the ratio between the nave and the aisle being 4:1.

The length of the nave, from the curve of the stūpa to the colonnade in the vestibule, is twice the height of the chamber. One would now expect that the two squares of the rectangular chamber would also be divided latitudinally into six units, which would give 2 × 6 bays. But the architect chose a latitudinal division into seven units, giving 2 × 7 bays. This new division was also used in the vertical section: the ratio between the height of the nave and that of the aisle is 7:3. Two units determine the upper edge of the bell-shaped capitals, and the height of the entire column (excluding the sculptures of mounted riders) corresponds to the diameter of the stūpa.

The façade of the rounded gable follows a grid of 32 × 32 square panels, the measurements of which, however, cannot be derived from those of the interior. The square of the façade is divided by a massive cornice into a lower part, comprising two storeys, and an upper one with miniature buildings. The centre of the horseshoe-shaped window is not in the centre of the square but one plan unit above the horizontal axis.

During the height of the period of Hīnayāna architecture a vestibule was sometimes added in front of the sanctum, so that on entering one should not step out of the glaring sunlight straight into the twilight of the hall. At Kārlī the vestibule terminates in a two-tiered colonnade. Only priests and monks could approach the vestibule and the main chamber along the axis. Laymen were permitted to enter the chaitya-hall only through the doors in the aisles.

The form of the prayer-hall was modified for the last time under the Gupta emperors, whose patronage enabled many Buddhist monasteries to enjoy a new flourishing period. The vihāras at Ajantā were no longer able to accommodate the rapidly growing number of monks. For this reason dwellings were first built for them on a grand scale; later it was found that there was no longer enough room in the old chaitya-halls for communal prayers and confessions. Therefore between A.D. 550 and 600 two small halls were hewn out of the rocky slope; these bear the imprint of the theistic form of Buddhism, Mahāyāna.

In the interior of these caves the figure of the Buddha as God emerges from the raised base of the stūpa. His image is repeated in various 'mudrās' (ritual gestures) and in all sizes on façades, on capitals and friezes, and above them. The medhi and anda sink to the level of a lavishly ornamented frame for the image of the Enlightened One, and it is hardly possible any longer to identify the formal origins of the harmikā and chattravalī. Hīnayāna architecture, which had been shaped by the spirit of monastic austerity, was now subjected to the influence of courtly art and the renewed spread of iconolatry among the Hindus.

Vihāras (monasteries)

Before a prayer-hall was carved out of the rock of a mountain, a small cave near the prospective building site was carved out as a dwelling-place for the priest-architects who had to supervise the progress of the work. An 'architect's office' of this kind consisted merely of a few dormitory cells, grouped around a small corridor.

When all the work on the prayer-hall had been completed, the labourers began to carve spacious dwellings for the monks out of the rock. Wooden monastic buildings again served as the model. A Hīnayāna monastery consists as a rule of a large rectangular room with dormitory cells arranged on three sides. In contrast to later Mahāyāna monasteries, there are no colonnades on the façade or in the main chamber. The structural model was a single-storeyed house built around an atrium, with rooms that opened directly on to the court or the garden of the monastery.

The Mahāyāna monasteries at Ajantā exemplify the development of the ground-plan of the monastery. In the neighbourhood of the chaitya-halls several exact copies of 'structive' vihāras were hewn out of the rock. The prototypes differed from those of the Hīnayāna vihāras in that the dormitory cells were not situated directly around the central court of the monastery but opened on to an interpolated covered gallery.

When the structural model was translated underground, to a rock-cut monastery, there was no possibility of including a garden, and its place is taken by a spacious rectangular assembly hall. All the architectural elements of the cloister, however, were faithfully imitated: columns, imposts to apportion the pressure, purlins and rafters. On the other hand, the ceiling of the assembly hall is level, since this took the place of the original open court. The cloister is entered from outside by way of an entrance verandah, which is separated from it by a wall with windows. On the outside the verandah is bounded by a colonnade on the flat part of the rock. In the interior the monks' cells opposite the entrance side are transformed into shrines containing images. In the middle cell there is always a statue of the Buddha, larger than life-size.

When we compare the ground-plans and vertical sections of the chaitya-hall and the vihāra, it appears that the simple form of the monastery cannot match the bold treatment of space in the prayer-hall. And yet these two types of monument are akin in the sequence of verandah, gallery and a main room surrounded by columns. In the chaitya-hall the barrel-vaulting resolves the architectural members of the lower floor and seems to open up the chamber towards the top (e.g. at Kārlī, where the stūpa appears to stand in an open court); in the vihāra, on the other hand, the flat ceiling is covered by geometric and figurative ornaments. These bear no relation to the adjoining architectural elements. Instead they are intended to afford the assembly hall a sense of airiness, such as was produced by the blossoming monastery garden, in contrast to the darkness of the monks' cells.

Ground-plan and section of Buddhist cave monastery no. 2 at Ajantā

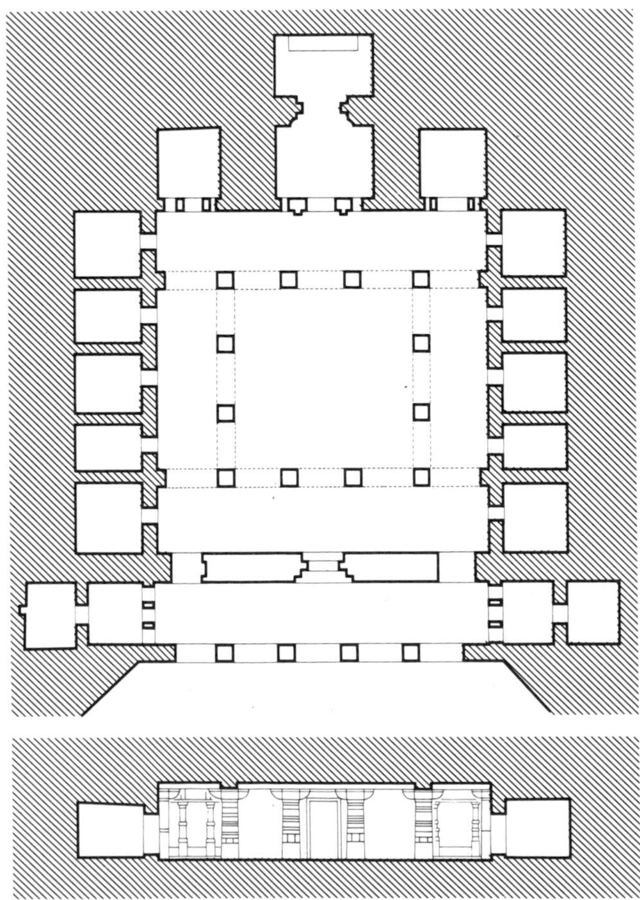

In the chaitya-hall the aisles are continued along the apse and the entrance side; the gallery of the vihāra performs its function at similar points: the point where the faithful enter the monastery and the point where they stand in veneration before the image of the Buddha. The worshipper's gaze is no longer directed into the chamber, towards a stūpa, which in its central situation symbolizes the laws governing the cosmos; instead his gaze is directed towards one of the cells, in which stands the image of the Redeemer who, like Christ, 'is among them' (Matt. xxviii. 20).

The aisles of the chaitya-hall correspond to the gallery of the vihāra, and the vestibule to the verandah. This is not to say that these two concepts of spatial treatment have a certain common origin. The only point of importance is that in both of them, although the functions they fulfil are different, the architect adopted the motifs of an open space, surrounding galleries and a vestibule in front. This is a basic Indian concept, which is featured in the catushālā dwelling-house, the houses at Mohenjo-daro, the monastery, the stūpa hall – and, last but not least, also in the typical metropolitan hotel of nineteenth-century Europe.

Buddhism owed its popularity among the lower classes of the population 'inter alia' to its rejection of the caste system and other Aryan traditions. In Mahāyāna the differences between Buddhism and Hinduism gradually became more and more blurred, until finally the former was absorbed by the Hinduism from which it had originally sprung. When that stage was reached, the Buddhist architectural tradition in India came to an end.

Plates

Somnāthpur

109 The Keshava temple, dating from the 3rd century A.D., seen from the entrance to the temple compound.

110 The socle of the cella wall is pierced by a gutter. The water mixed with fragrant scents with which the cult image is cleansed daily runs through this gutter into a basin, and is then channelled through a subterranean conduit out of the temple enclosure.

111 Diagonal view from the south-west of the main shrine in the east (left), the mandapa (centre) and the southern shrine (right).

112 The star-shaped ground-plan of the cella is repeated at every level.

113 The stellar form of the ground-plan can be clearly identified even in the pointed towers above the cella.

114 The repetition of architectonic forms on a reduced scale is one of the most popular motifs in the reliefs of this temple.

115 Detail of a window carved from soft soapstone.

116 The cella containing the image of the god Keshava, seen from the vestibule.

117 Some columns in the vestibule were turned, if they were of soft stone; others were star-shaped in cross-section, in imitation of the ground-plan.

Mount Ābū

118 The Jain temples.

119 Roof ornaments: variations on the theme of the tiered pyramid.

120 The dancing pavilion of the Tejapāla temple, looking west towards the entrance.

121 The low cupola over the dancing pavilion consists of several marble courses, set horizontally and overlapping. All the visible surfaces are carved in filigree.

122 The court of the Tejapāla temple.

123 In front of the circle of cellas is a small ambulatory hall. Each architrave and each capital has been worked in the same way, with a file instead of a chisel.

124 Parts of the temple court were covered over when the dancing pavilion was built one hundred years after completion of the cella.

125 The columns which support the roof of the dancing pavilion are decorated with sculptures of dancing temple girls.

Khajurāho

126 The Kandāriya Mahādeo temple, dating from the 11th century, seen from the west.

127 View of the Kandāriya Mahādeo temple (left) and the Kali-devi Jagadamba temple (right), from the north-east. Where the palaces of the Chandella kings once stood there are now only the few clay huts that comprise the village of Khajurāho.

128 Around the rathas of the main temple (shikhara) run bands of reliefs with figures. Celestial nymphs, the saints and gods of the legends are here assembled as if taking part in the circumambulatory rite around the sanctum.

129 The shikhara from the south. The basic form of the temple tower, a parabola, recurs in these miniature shikharas.

130 The mahā-mandapa (right) and the gallery around the cella (left) are lit from the verandahs above. Between them are representations of mithuna couples.

131 Detail of the south-western corner of the temple.

132 Detail of one of the celestial nymphs, of which there are more than a thousand.

The Kandāriya Mahādeo temple at Khajurāho
Ground-plan and elevation 1:250

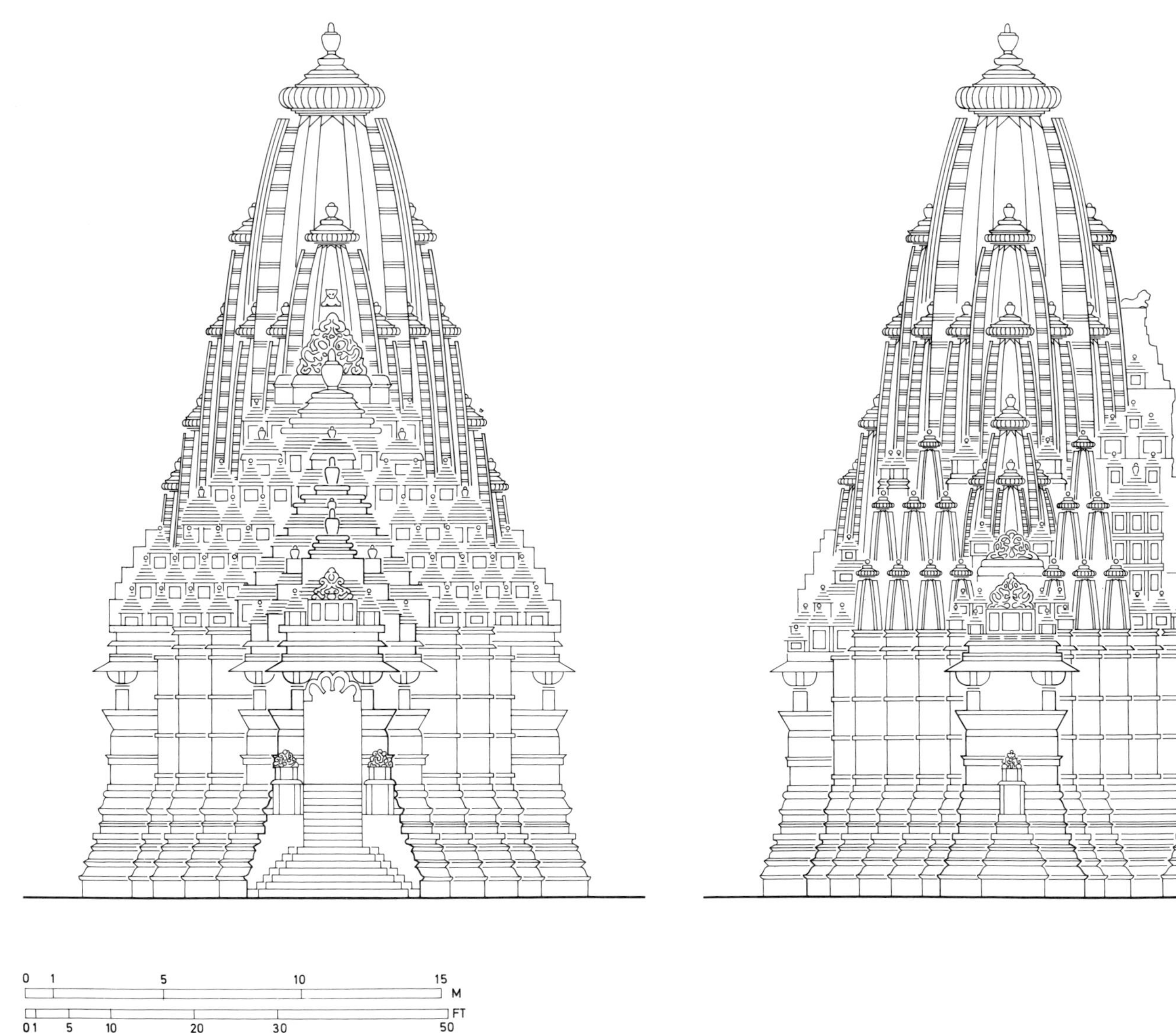

1 Garbha-griha
2 Interior pradakshinā-patha
3 Mandapa
4 Artha-mandapa

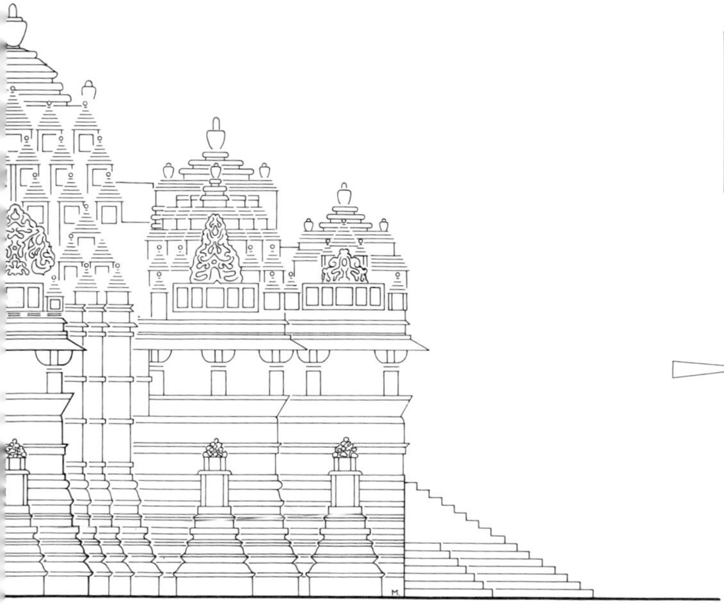

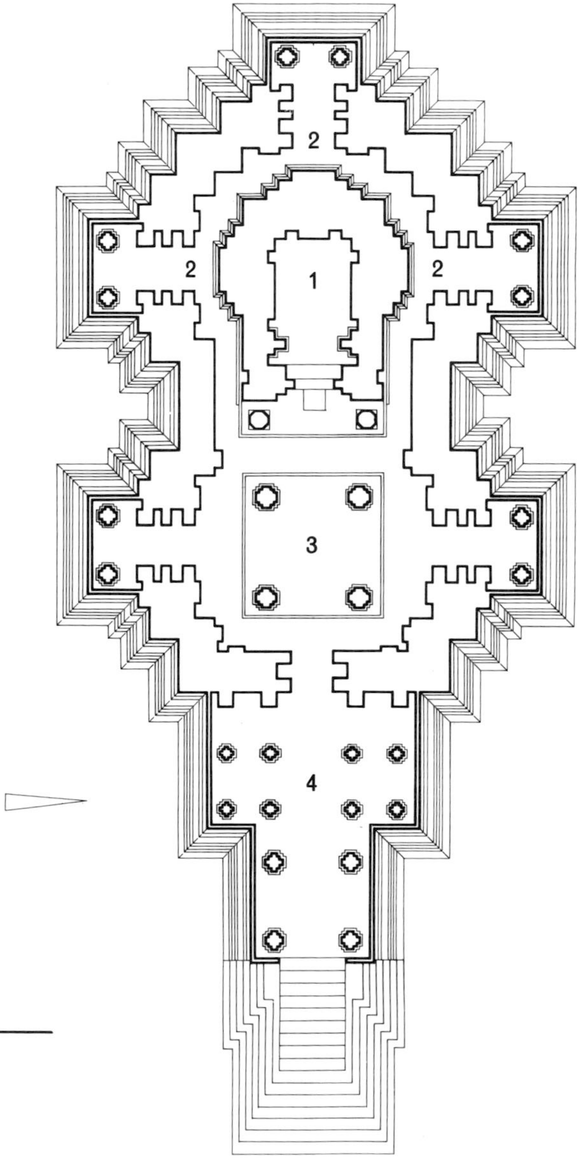

Notes

Somnāthpur

The idea of the Supreme Principle, called Brahman, as a trinity is reflected in the three main divinities of the Hindu pantheon. Occasionally this triple division is applied to each of these three gods. For example, in the caves at Elephanta near Bombay there is a three-faced representation of Shiva as creator, preserver and destroyer. The sanctuary at Somnāthpur, too, is dedicated to three incarnations of one god of the fundamental trinity. Vishnu appears as Janardana, as Krishna, and – in the central shrine – as Keshava.

According to an inscription on a stone plaque in the entrance hall, the village of Somnāthpur and the sanctuary were founded by a general in the service of the Hoysala dynasty, by the name of Somanatha; it was originally called Somanathapura (city of Somanatha). The temple was built of light-coloured steatite (soapstone), which was quarried in the immediate vicinity. This soft material can be cut and also carved with ease, but once it has been exposed to the air it becomes hard and acquires a greasy black lustre. Chalukya style is confined to this region, and its development was brought to an end by the invading Mohammedans at the beginning of the fourteenth century.

Mount Ābū

In the temple cities of the Gujarat district – Girnar, Palitāna and Ābū – the Jain temples as a rule also follow the canon of form and proportions of the Hindu nagara style. But in contrast to the Hindu temples they are built of marble. Wealthy merchants from Gujarat were able to afford such a costly material and to pay for its transport to the site. When the temple was founded they set up a committee to look after it. Most Jain sanctuaries are therefore far better preserved than Hindu ones (except for Madurai, which was restored ten years ago with the aid of generous contributions). Even today the Jain community of Ābū looks after the regular cleaning of the gleaming white marble monuments. Some of the sculptures and reliefs are stiff repetitions of a few basic forms. Considered as individual works, they are often of little artistic value, but they have been incorporated into the architectonic frame with extraordinary skill, so that their shortcomings are not noticed. Even today the stone-masons of Ābū fashion with chisel and file the same figures that were made for the temples in the eleventh and twelfth centuries. It is thus hardly possible to date individual sculptures.

Khajurāho

The interest taken in the temple and capital city of Khajurāho stems primarily from the reputation of the erotic sculptures, the representations of mithuna on the temple walls. But the rendering of loving couples is only one aspect of the pre-Aryan fertility cults which are deeply rooted in Hinduism. The temple tower and assembly hall are often referred to in ancient texts as bride and bridegroom; and of the Hindu trinity (Brahmā, Vishnu and Shiva) it is Shiva who is worshipped first and foremost, and his symbol is the phallus, called lingam.

The vāstu-purusha mandala, a square rendering of the world and the abodes of the gods, determined the groundplan of the temple, the arrangement of the miniature shikharas around the central tower, and also the 'embryo' form of one temple. This 'embryo' was a square casket in gold, the size of which was fixed by the proportions of the sanctuary. In this casket the mandala of the temple was drawn; golden fillets were incorporated as dividing-lines between the pādas, forming the several compartments. Into the Brahmā-sthāna were placed precious stones and the attributes of the deity; the adjoining pādas contained four different lotus blossoms, corn, pigments and certain metals. When the temple was being built, on one 'immaculate night' the priest performed the 'rite of fertilization' and immured this 'embryo' in the wall of the garbha-griha. Many more connections between Hindu religious rites and ancient fertility cults could be mentioned. It is only with this background in mind that one can do justice to the sculptures of Khajurāho. Their artistry and craftsmanship prevent them from being regarded simply as symptomatic of this undoubtedly decadent epoch.

132

The Keshava temple at Somnāthpur

Ground-plan and vertical section 1:500

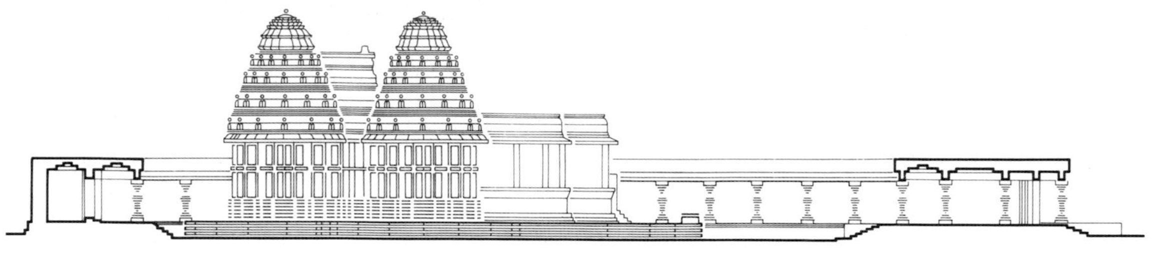

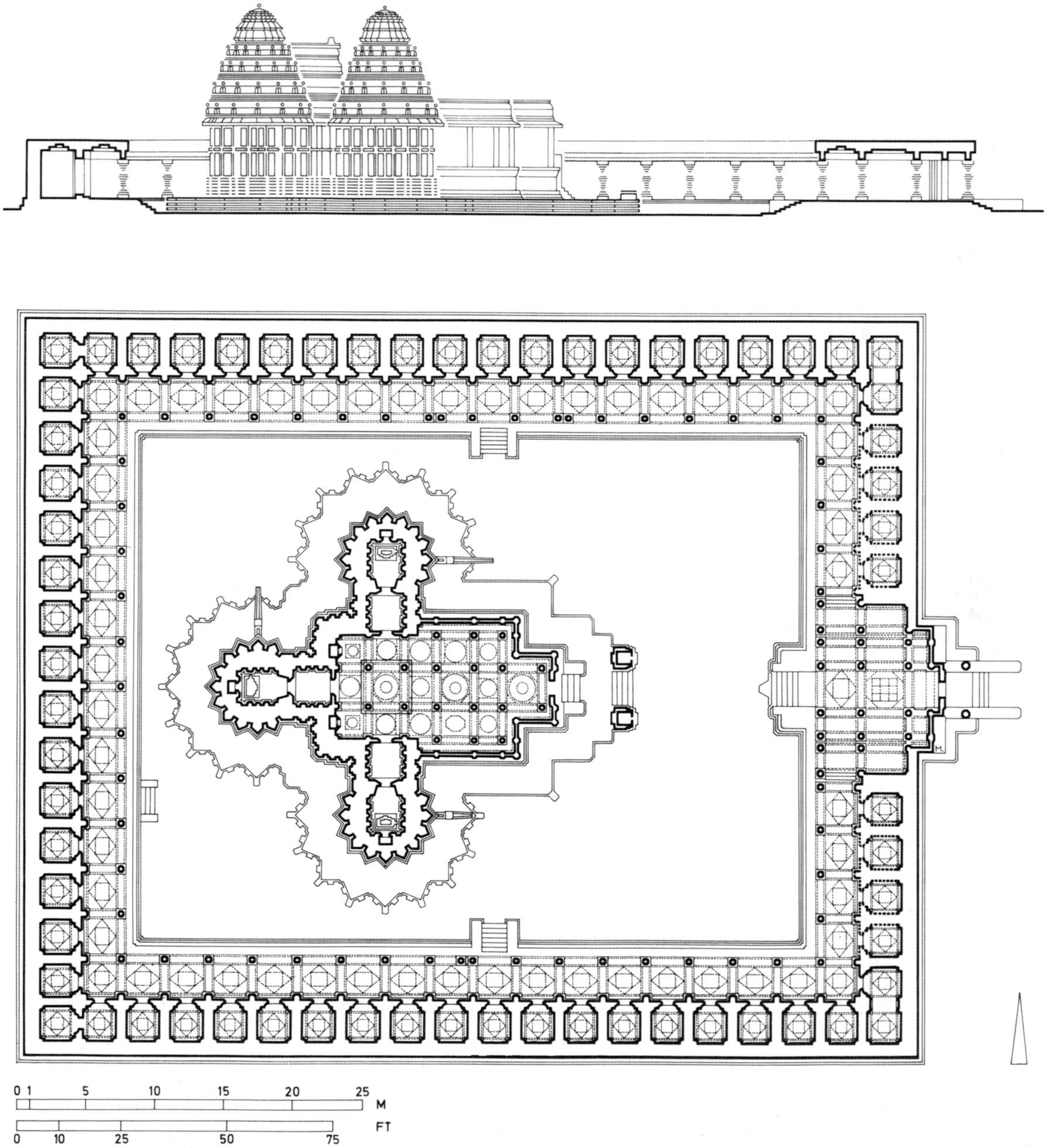

0 1 5 10 15 20 25 M

0 10 25 50 75 FT

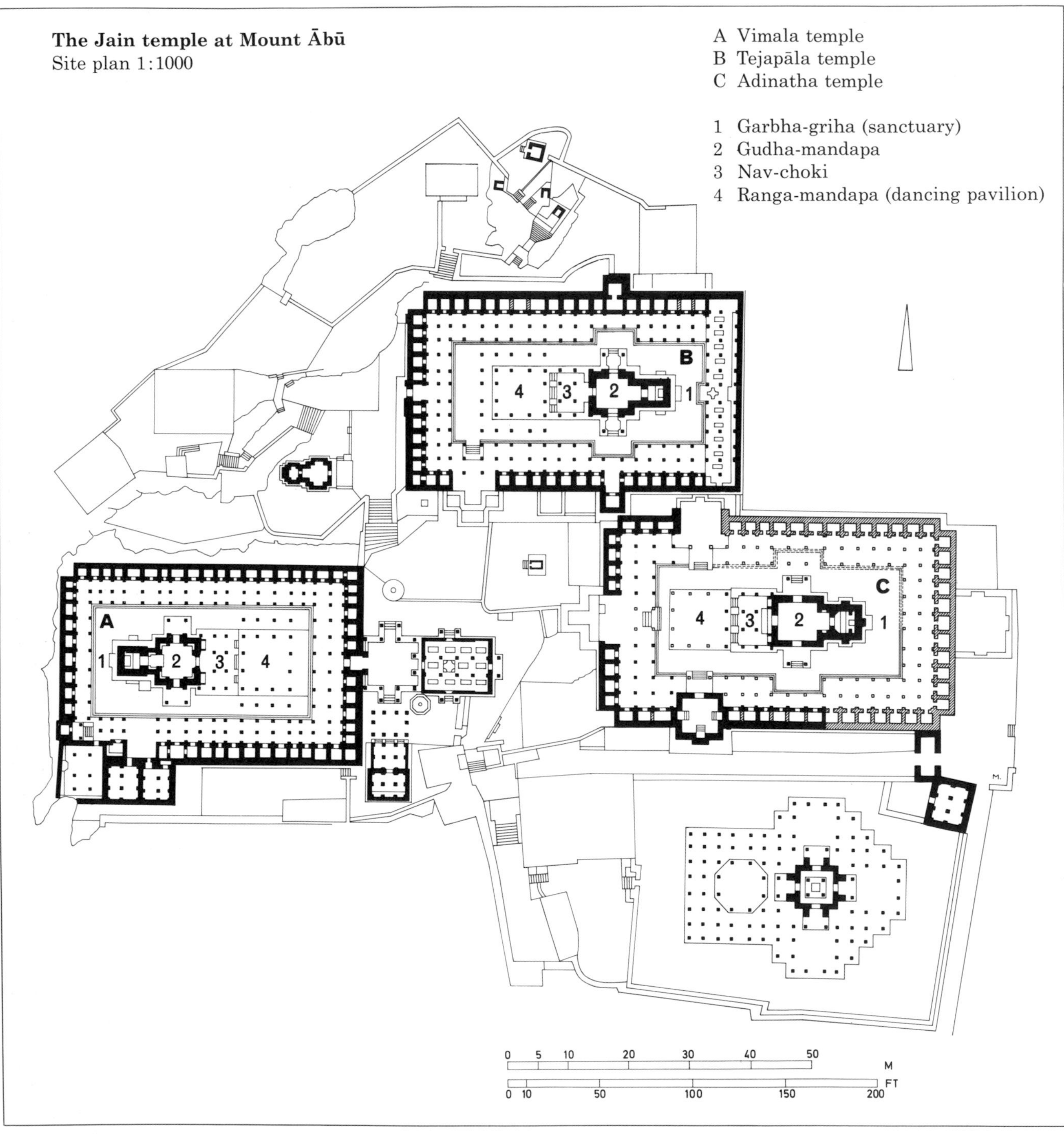

The Jain temple at Mount Ābū
Site plan 1:1000
A Vimala temple
B Tejapāla temple
C Adinatha temple
1 Garbha-griha (sanctuary)
2 Gudha-mandapa
3 Nav-choki
4 Ranga-mandapa (dancing pavilion)
A
B
C
1
2
3
4
M.
0 5 10 20 30 40 50
M
FT
0 10 50 100 150 200

4. Hindu and Jain Sanctuaries

The oldest surviving Hindu temples were built by the Chalukyas at Aihole during the Gupta era, i.e. between A.D. 350 and 650. The Lādh Khān and Durgā temples, to take two particularly characteristic examples, are copies of previously existing communal buildings. The ground-plan and vertical section of the Lādh Khān temple show that it is modelled upon a contemporary village council hall, whereas the form of the Durgā temple is taken from that of the Buddhist chaitya-hall. In both cases the need to elevate the temple above its mundane environment led to the erection of a small tower over the central point of the building (Lādh Khān temple) or over the cella (Durgā temple).

In early Hindu society there was no activity, such as a religious service, in which the whole community took part as a body. This was ruled out by the stratification into castes and by the view that the individual believer alone could become cognizant of the Supreme Being and identify himself with him by personal effort and by closely observing rules that applied solely to him and his clan. Religious rites were therefore carried out at the small altar which existed in every house. Even Hindu monastic communities differ from Christian or Buddhist ones in that each member has to find his own way to Brahman without any assistance from his fellow-monks. The monastery was indeed the residence of persons who shared common beliefs, and who held vigorous theological disputes, but it was not considered valuable to congregate to praise God. Meditation was possible only in solitude.

For these reasons the early types of temple proved unsuited to further development. The common people were satisfied with the private altar-room in their dwelling-houses; only the aristocracy could give the stimulus to build monumental shrines for images.

From the seventh century A.D. onwards two stylistic tendencies can be distinguished in temple construction, which, developing along independent lines, can be followed throughout the history of Indian architecture up to the present time. In north India temples were built mainly in the Indo-Aryan, or so-called

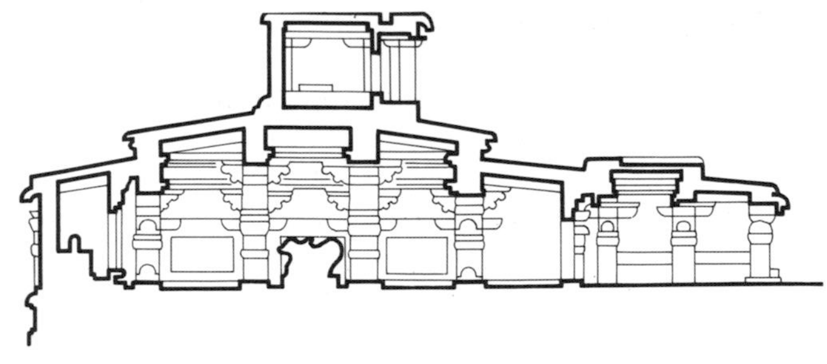

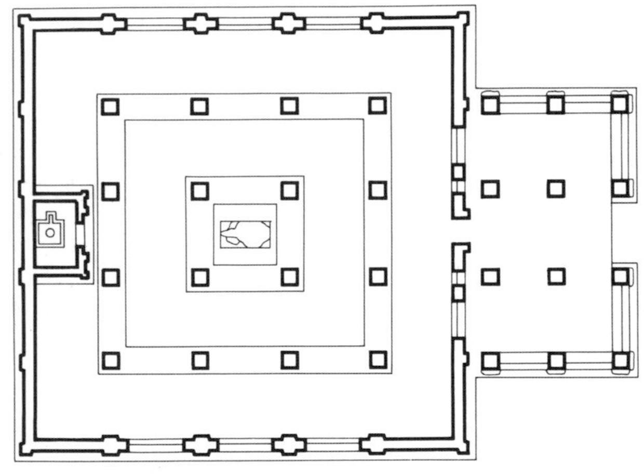

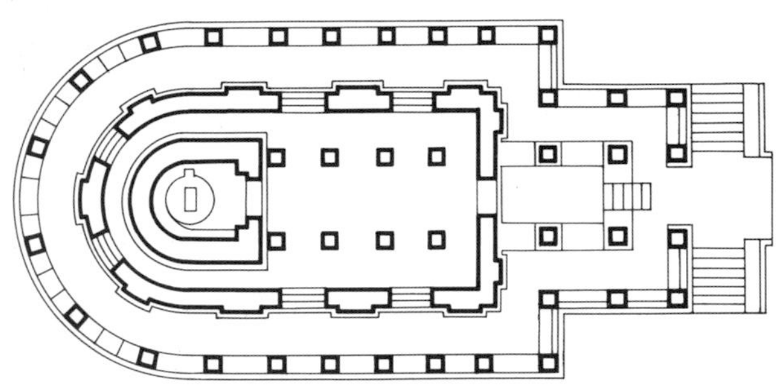

Early types of Hindu temple
a) Ground-plan and vertical section of the Lādh Khān temple (450B.C.)
b) Ground-plan of the Durgā temple (550B.C.)

'nāgara' style; in south India we find temples built in the 'dravida' style. The formal canon of both tendencies can be derived from the Aihole temples, even though we cannot assign them clearly to any particular category. When the Chalukya dynasty, whose capital city was situated in turn at Aihole, Bādāmī and Pattadkal, collapsed, the construction of stone temples was developed many hundreds of miles to the south or to the north, in the capitals of dark-skinned Dravidian or fair-skinned Aryan rulers.

Early dravida style

If one travels through the country around Vijayanagar in south India, one is led to assume that the form of south Indian temples was influenced by natural prototypes. In this area, where a powerful Hindu kingdom was founded in the fourteenth century, the terrain seems to consist of enormous blocks of flint; rounded boulders are heaped up to form scree-covered hills; often some of these rocks lie on top of one another, as though piled up by some mysterious spirit. These natural towers have at the base a flint several metres thick, while the stones become progressively smaller towards the top. Even today some Indians believe that the gods have their seat on the pinnacles of these marvels of nature. If there was enough room, these towers were crowned by a small temple. Thus the traveller to Vijayanagar passes through avenues of temples several miles long. Their tops, painted white and red, stretch from end to end of the horizon.

In the Chalukya kingdom the type of temple evolved from communal meeting halls was adhered to until the ninth century A.D. The cella and vestibule formed a single architectural unit. But everywhere else in India during this early period of temple architecture preference was given to the free-standing cella not connected to an assembly hall. In the Pallava kingdom, at the southern tip of the sub-continent, the seventh-century king Mahendravarman I began to employ stone columns in temples. Later his son, Narasimhavarman I, who conquered the Chalukya cities, became acquainted with the stone temples of Aihole, Bādāmī and Pattadkal. On his return to his capital at Kanchīpuram he decided to erect temples that would vie with those of the Chalukyas, constructed of layers of rough stones and then finely worked.

The rathas of Mahaballipuram

Narasimhavarman chose as his site the town of Mahaballipuram, situated on the coast and honeycombed with granite cliffs. It seemed a wasteful procedure first to hew the stones in the Chalukya manner, then to transport them to the site with great difficulty, and finally to re-assemble them there. He therefore chose a favourably situated granite ridge and invited his architects, in competition with artisans brought from the conquered Chalukya kingdom, to come there and to run through the various possible forms that a cella could take. Their models were reed-roofed dwelling-houses, portable wooden shrines, Buddhist chaitya-halls, and multi-tiered Buddhist monasteries. Since this was evidently an experiment, they adapted the scale of their efforts to the natural formation of the rock. It was not thought important to keep strictly to the geometric form. If a recess in the rock made it necessary, the plan was adjusted to accommodate such an irregularity.

These model temples remained unfinished. Whether they were ever consecrated and used remains uncertain. The cap-stones which are placed on the apex of a Hindu temple upon consecration are still to be seen next to the shrines, ready to be laid in position.

Mahaballipuram decided the form which the monumental temple in south India was to assume during the centuries that followed. The working of monolithic rathas was abandoned once the external appearance of the various forms of building was clear down to the last detail. As for the interior, the king's decision for or against a particular type was immaterial, since any departure from the traditional undecorated cubic cella would have been sacrilege. The architects did indeed make an effort to provide the exterior with a logical complement within, but in most models they refrained from any attempt to modify the cubic form of the cella in order to bring about a formal or functional equivalence with the exterior.

1. Draupadī ratha

It was tempting to preserve the unpretentious form of the portable wooden shrine with its grass roof, because if this were reproduced on a larger scale it would afford an interior area convenient for circumambulation of the cult object. The monolithic shrine of Draupadī ratha does not conceal the influence of its prototype. The beasts of burden that used to carry such portable shrines are suggested as a form for the base. The curved thatched roof, which despite its volume was just right for a little wooden temple, looks intolerably clumsy when translated into stone. Since this roof was a compact architectural element with fixed proportions, it seemed impossible to employ it in a large stone temple or to enlarge it by adding more elements of the same kind. Perhaps the architects realized that in a temple constructed of stone blocks – we shall call such buildings 'structive' in contrast to monolithic ones – a projecting and overhanging roof would be a very difficult proposition.

2. Sahadeva ratha

An alternative model to that of the thatched hut was the barrel roof of the Buddhist chaitya-hall. For the first time the architects tried to blend the vaulted roof, terminating in an apse, with the theologically inspired form of the tiered pyramid. The barrel-vaulted ceiling, however, presupposes an elongated

a) The Draupadī ratha at Mahaballipuram is modelled on a small wooden shrine
b) The Sahadeva ratha combines a tiered pyramid, barrel roof and rounded apse

a)

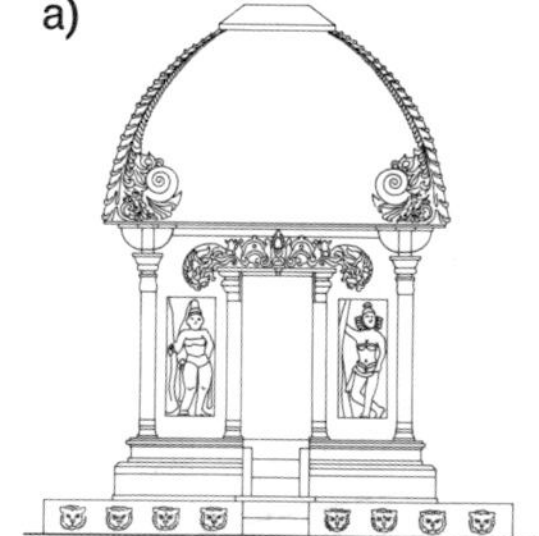

b)

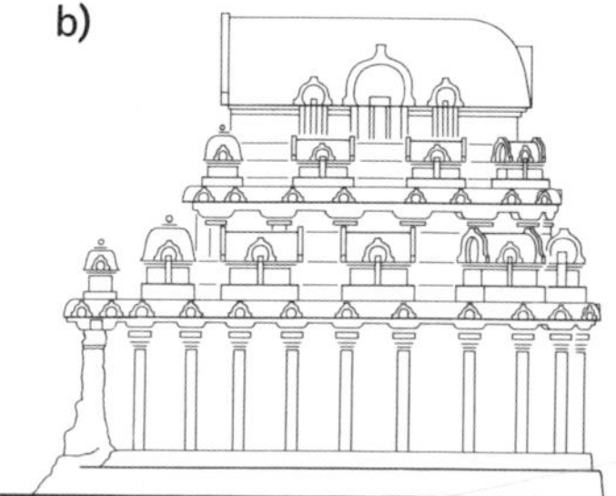

body. In conformity with the Buddhist prototypes, the entrance was sited in the front wall, opposite the apse.

This emphasis on human action is typical of Buddhist architecture; but the Hindu sthapati, for whom the temple is a manifestation of the supreme principle of order, cannot but find such a point of reference unacceptable.

3. Bhīma ratha

Here, too, an attempt is made to adhere to the rich tradition of the barrel roof. If one dispensed with the apse on one side and suggested a pillared gallery, one would take two big steps towards making this type of building more suited to a monumental Hindu temple. But its defect was that it would hardly be feasible to place a large barrel roof on narrow columns. (In the model the upper storeys rest upon the core of the monolith, which with good reason has not been carved out.) Moreover, there was no clearly defined place for the cult image in this rectangular building.

4. Dharmarāja ratha

This model is the most successful effort to do justice to all the formal, cosmological and ritual requirements involved in the construction of a temple. Its size could be varied, because it consisted of any number of equal parts, which could be put together like building-blocks. The square plan, not oriented in any particular direction, obviated the chief defect of Buddhist temples (in the eyes of Hindu architects): the regimented sequence of all architectural elements, leading up to the stūpa instead of radiating outwards from it in all directions. There is no discrepancy here between the form of the exterior and of the interior.

The monolithic Bhīma ratha at Mahaballipuram has a barrel roof

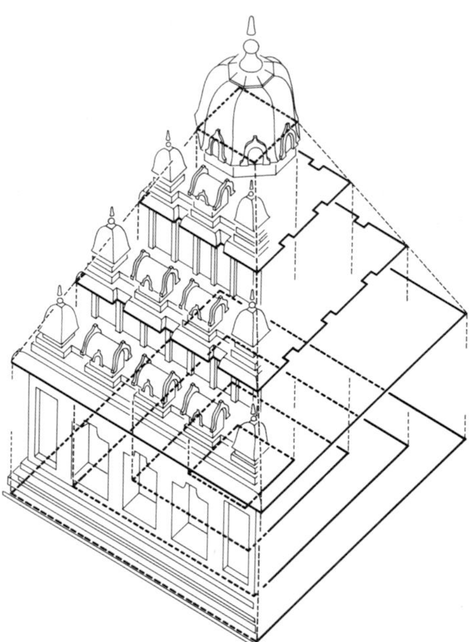

The spatial mandala in the Dharmarāja ratha

The pyramidal arrangement of miniature temples reflects the ancient myth of Meru, the cosmic mountain. If we were to look at the temple from the air, we would see how in the seventh century A.D. architects, with consummate skill, were able to translate into their own idiom the doctrine of the mandala, the magic diagram. Initiates could not see, as we can perceive by means of a sectional diagram, how the monument is built in accordance with the most important of all grid plans in south India. The outer limits of the tiered roofs and of the octagonal domes contain a central Brahmā-sthāna, and rings of deities, humans and demons. It is an integral diagram, transposed into spatial dimensions.

Classical dravida style

Rājasimha (A.D. 690–715) was the first ruler who, after the period of war and confusion was over, had enough leisure to draw the consequences from these experiments with the series of monolithic temples. Borrowing the form and structure of the Dharmarāja ratha, he erected a number of 'structive' temples in his capital city of Kanchīpuram and the port of Mahaballipuram. The three most important ones are the Kailāsanāth and Vaikuntaperumalai temples in the former city and the shore temple in the latter.

The circumstances in which the shore temple was built made it necessary to deviate in certain respects from the standard ground-plan and vertical section. The principal shrine has its entrance on the eastern side. This conforms to the rule that a sanctuary should face the rising sun. At the same time this orientation towards the sea (Mahaballipuram is on the east coast) made possible a mutual relationship between the sanctuary and ships sailing into the harbour. In the circuit wall of the temple an opening was left at a point that could not be reached from the shore, through which mariners could catch a direct glimpse of the cella. The cella contains a lingam and is therefore dedicated to Shiva. To the west of the main tower is a small shrine with an image of Vishnu in its cella. We may recall the rules in the old manuals to the effect that a temple should face the city, or that at least one divine image must face in this direction, if the cosmic laws require such an orientation. Presumably such considerations were still borne in mind at Mahaballipuram in the seventh century; this temple, which faces away from the city, has a little temple attached to it facing in the opposite direction.

Another characteristic of this temple is that its courtyards could be partially flooded. Remains of conduits have been found through which fresh water could be channelled to the temple. The water was then passed through pipes into shallow basins situated around the cult rooms. The excess water was let out into the sea on the east side of the sanctuary. Why this complex installation was built remains uncertain: possibly the form of the temple was influenced by ancient snake and water cults. Apart from Kārlī and Mahaballipuram we do not know of any Indian sanctuaries in which water played a part in determining their layout.

The most conspicuous feature of the shore temple is its unusually tall tower. The exaggerated height of individual tiers could be attributed to a whim of the architect or of his royal patron; but it seems more probable, first, that esoteric reasons prescribed a particular number of tiers (the texts say that their number must not be fixed arbitrarily), and, secondly, that it was desired to make the temple a landmark visible from afar.

At night, when the temple was not visible to mariners, a light was lit on one of the tall stone pillars to the east of the temple. Ships approaching the coast could correct their course by reference to this temple lamp and a beacon situated on a rocky ridge inland.

The local population have a legend that at one time several such temples lined the shore at Mahaballipuram. At ebb tide some regular heaps of stone are indeed visible under the surface of the water. Why only one temple in this series should have survived for more than 1200 years we do not know. The destructive action of the sea air, of 1200 monsoons and 1200 dry seasons, and of the shifting sand dunes have worn away all the contours of the building, but have not ruined its stately structure. The builders were relatively inexperienced in erecting stone temples. However, the basic principle of Hindu architecture has been very well preserved: this is the arrangement of the stone blocks in horizontal layers, which is derived not from speculations in the field of statics but from theological considerations. All structural elements, except for a few supporting beams, are brought into play only when exposed to pressure. Thereby the best quality of stone, its ability to withstand pressure, is exploited in a rational way.

The dwarf structures on the tiers of the pyramid have led some historians of architecture to the theory that the dravida pyramidal roofs were only small-scale reductions of multi-tiered buildings. In accordance with this theory P. K. Acharya, in his edition of the manual Mānasāra, envisaged the existence of pyramid-shaped monasteries with as many as twelve storeys. But both on structural and on functional grounds one must dismiss as inapt the notion of a building consisting of one layer after another of pillared halls, diminishing in size towards the top. According to the 'Mānasāra' one can enlarge a building supported by columns 'ad libitum' by placing it upon another pillared hall. The author of this ancient manual presumably knew that one can make a pyramid of any height by placing one stone slab upon another, and simply transferred this idea to an architectural context. Since, however, he evidently had no empirical knowledge of the statics of a multi-tiered building, it seems improbable that the pyramids so fondly described ever existed in fact. Such descriptions of multi-tiered buildings are either ultimate ideals or allegorical interpretations of celestial structures – of the cosmic mountain Meru. The equivalent in Buddhist architecture is the multi-tiered honorary umbrella over the stūpa.

In the north the Chalukya kingdom bordered on that of the Pallavas. In the middle of the eighth century A.D. this dynasty was superseded by that of the Rāshtrakūtas. The power of the Pallavas had also passed its zenith. Around A.D. 900 the hitherto insignificant Chola family succeeded in destroying the Pallava kingdom and within a century had brought all the districts south of the river Krishnā under its sway. Both the Rāshtrakūtas and the Cholas, when at the height of their power, founded a sanctuary in dravida style: the Rāshtrakūtas built the Kailāsa temple at Elūrā at the end of the eighth century A.D., and the Cholas built the Brihadeshvara temple at Tanjore in approximately A.D. 1000.

Elūrā

At Mahaballipuram the Pallavas had carved the exteriors of model temples out of granite. Simultaneously they had dug chambers in vertical rocky cliffs, copying Buddhist prototypes. Never, however, do they seem to have felt the need to execute a complete structure as a monolith. We may find it hard to understand this sharp distinction between the interior and exterior of a building. In our era, when architects, at least in theory, stress the interdependence of both aspects, we should clearly bear in mind that classical Indian sacred buildings were primarily intended as allegories. The mountain of Kailāsa is the seat of Shiva, translated into geometric and plastic architectonic forms. Such a concept leaves little room for considerations such as which form will do most justice to the material, or how the interior and exterior will interact. The central point of a temple is always the little cubic cella. In the course of time its stone casing takes on different forms in various districts, but without affecting the shape of the interior.

The sanctuary of Elūrā represents the first attempt to translate a complete temple, with all its external and internal features, into rock. The model chosen was the Virupaksha temple at Pattadkal, which in turn was influenced by Pallava temples. It will be recalled that in the Chalukya kingdom, in contrast to north and south India, the cella was joined directly on to the mandapa. This combination re-appears at Elūrā (see plan, p. 59). In this ancient place of pilgrimage for Buddhists, Hindus and Jains the builders chose a rocky slope, the inclination of which corresponded to the terracing of the monument, which has a low entrance door at the base and culminates in the main tower above the cella. The carving of this complex structure posed completely new problems for the architects, surveyors and sculptors. They had to reproduce single- and multi-storeyed areas, bridges and entrance halls, with columns in the interior and free-standing pillars in the court. This presupposed very precise planning, to fix the location of each architectural element. The objective was to transform the rock into an image of Shiva's mountain abode which would last for ever. It should be borne in mind that in this vast monument there are no architraves to give support and no joints. None of the chambers in the interior was formed by building walls. The process of 'building' could be called 'reductive' in contrast to the additive method used in 'structive' temples. Nothing illustrates better our helplessness when confronted with this phenomenon of anti-tectonic architecture than the lack of an appropriate vocabulary.

When we were considering the chaitya-halls and monasteries at Ajantā or Kārlī, we had the opportunity to bring different caves into association with one another. The monolithic rathas at Mahaballipuram could be visualized as sculptures on an architectonic theme. But neither of these ways of comprehending unfamiliar phenomena by reference to familiar ones can be applied at Elūrā. If we want to understand the Kailāsa temple we must try to follow the ideas in the mind of the architect. At the time when the donor, Krishna I, was on the throne it was already common practice to build temples in stone, wood or stucco. The priest-architects must have felt it undignified to have to struggle with this material and to face the uncertainties of a structure that was to have dimensions, and fulfil religious ambitions, on a scale hitherto unknown. They must also have felt it improper to break up the rock until it was reduced to dimensions compatible with human strength, precisely because their intention was to create an image of God that would be beyond the human scale. It seemed to them more appropriate to adopt the 'reductive' method used in sculpture, whereby only what is inessential would be hewn away, but the actual substance of the temple would remain untouched by human hand.

As the ground-plan shows, Elūrā has the typical south Indian sequence of architectural bodies, which was to be adopted without modification during the centuries that followed. Inside the entrance gate (gopura) is a small pavilion to accommodate the image of Shiva's sacred mount, the bull ('nandi-mandapa'). The twilight of a spacious pillared hall (mandapa) prepares the believer for the cella (gribha-griha), which is enveloped in darkness. In the centre of this is the lingam, the phallic representation of Shiva. Flanking the main tower ('vimāna') are doors which lead from the mandapa to the processional path (pradakshinā-patha). The miniature buildings are a motif that recurs on the ancillary shrines bordering the processional path.

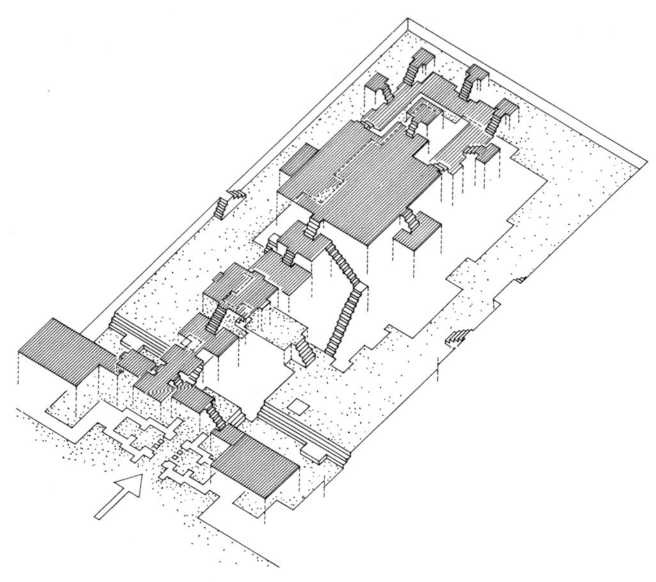

The Kailāsa temple at Elūrā. Layout on two levels. The upper level was presumably reserved for priests and kings

Strangely enough, this sequence has been transferred to the upper storey; the lower storey consists of the massive base upon which the temple stands. This differentiation enhances the noble impression conveyed by the entire complex, but also has the consequence that on entering at the lower-storey level one cannot walk toward the temple along the axis, past the nandi-mandapa, and can only reach the level of the actual rooms in the temple by way of a narrow flight of steps on either side of the mandapa. Here, too, the architect adhered to a traditional structure, although this was no longer in keeping with the new functions of the monument. The reason why the actual entrance was moved to a level which bore no proper relation to the sequence of rooms was that laymen were allotted the court around the base, whereas the upper storey was occupied solely by priests and by the king.

Tanjore

The south Indian temple tower attains its final glory at Tanjore, about 1000 kilometres south of Elūrā. In Chapter II we have already briefly discussed the ground-plan of this sanctuary, and may now consider its vertical section. Every dravida temple tower consists of a lower part with vertical walls and an upper part shaped like a pyramid. This is true not only of the rathas, the shore temple and the Kailāsa temple, but also of the Brihadeshvara temple at Tanjore, built at the beginning of the eleventh century. But why should its lower part, the rectangular cube, have a two-storeyed façade? An explanation is afforded by the temples in the neighbouring district of Āndhra. As it developed, the lingam in the garbha-griha was represented in ever larger dimensions. The ritual ablutions, in the course of which Shiva's symbol had buttermilk and butter poured over it and was richly bedecked with flowers, could not be carried out if the tip could not be reached. For this reason architects began to erect in the cella a wooden gallery around the lingam, which might be as high as the roof of the chamber. Finally, the entire monument came to be executed in two storeys. The lower chamber continued to be used for the pradakshinā rite and the upper one for ablutions. This idea of a two-storeyed structure, conditioned by functional requirements, was adopted by the architects of Chola temples, although here the gallery was no longer employed for ablutions of the lingam, but was reserved as a place of meditation for pilgrims unable to take part in the pradakshinā rite in the garbha-griha. For this reason access to the upper storey was no longer gained from the cella itself but from the 'artha-mandapa'. At Tanjore the cella is two storeys high and the gallery is located above a second pradakshinā-patha in the interior. It has windows from which one can look down into the garbha-griha. The two storeys inside the temple led to a corresponding articulation of the façade.

In Chapter II we saw that the ground-plan is evidently based upon the padmagarbha mandala, comprising 16 × 16 pādas. The façades follow different rules of proportion, which can be worked out from the lowest course of the pyramidal tower. The miniature shrines show that the façade is articulated into six axes. The two axes in the centre are indicated by projecting horseshoe-shaped bays in the elongated barrel roof; the other four axes are symmetrical and run through the miniature shrines on either side. This division is continued in the vertical façades of the temple tower. Here the six axes of the miniature shrines are symmetrically aligned with the six niches containing images. The latter were of such proportions as to make the flanking pilasters equidistant from one another – in other words, the space between two niches is as wide as one niche. Only the top of the outermost pair of pilaster shafts is significantly broader. For this there is a simple reason: the pilasters project far beyond the miniature shrines. These salients are caused by a structural feature, the slop-

The 'conflict at the corners' on the temple at Tanjore
above: façade; below: part of ground-plan
A = axial point
b = width of axes of niches containing images
c = amount by which corner niches need to be widened

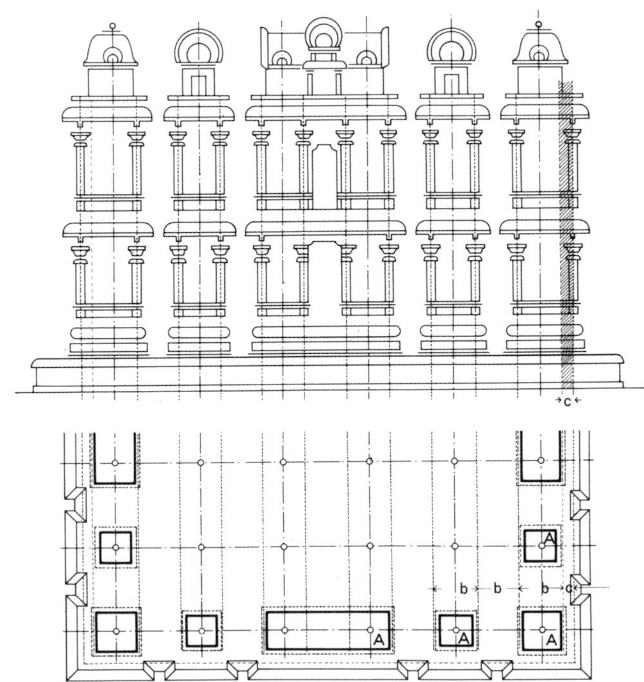

ing roof of the pyramid. Now if the distance between the niche and the point of its axis ('A') is greater than its breadth ('b'), there will be an inevitable conflict in the formation of the corner. The niche must be enlarged exactly by ('c'), the amount by which it is too far away from the point of its axis. The solution of this conflict preoccupied Indian architects of the sixth century B.C. as well as those of the eleventh century A.D. The former had for optical reasons placed a particularly broad architrave upon Doric columns. Thereby the triglyph frieze of the entablature was removed so far from the axis of the columns that the metope on the corner had to be enlarged. An example of this may also be seen in the basilica at Paestum.

In front of the vimāna there are short sections of wall, likewise two-storeyed, which could form the starting-point of a mandapa. But the completed mandapa does not belong to the original complex. The apertures at regular intervals along the base of the wall suggest that a wooden structure formerly stood in front of the stone temple tower.

The nandi-mandapa did not acquire its present form until the seventeenth century. Surprisingly enough, it is situated above the point of intersection between the diagonals of a square, which, together with the square already mentioned around the vimāna, defines the outer limits of the sanctuary. The arbitrary disposition of the ancillary shrines shows that the plan of the layout had been forgotten a few centuries after the main temple was built. We are therefore right to assume that by the time of the Chola rulers a nandi bull was to be found above the centre of the square.

Since the temple tower is some 70 metres high, it is a landmark visible from afar which dominates the city of Tanjore. In the sacred area itself all the columnar halls and ancillary shrines in front of it seem insignificant by comparison. The rooms in the interior of the tower are a disappointment, since they do not correspond in the slightest to the monumental dimensions of the exterior.

The miniature shrines on the lowest storey of the pyramid are as big as an ordinary Indian dwelling-house. They could have been entered through the doors in the axes of the façade if there had been a flight of steps up to this level. Even the uppermost storeys are still high enough for one to crawl into them. According to statements by a resident Brahmin, the double-shelled construction of the cella is not continued in the tower. The upper gallery ends in corbel-vaulting and only the cella area is repeated in all the storeys of the roof, becoming smaller and smaller. In former times this was where the treasures of the temple were kept. The exceptional height of the temple tower, however, cannot be explained by the need for a place to accommodate these treasure-chambers. King Rāja-rāja I, conscious of his power, apparently had it built as high as technical means permitted. Superlatives are in order not only in regard to the dimensions of the tower. The lingam in the sanctuary is by far the largest in India and also the cap-stone at the top of the terraced pyramid, which weighs 80 tons, is the largest stone slab ever to have been used in 'structive' architecture.

Late dravida style

During the first centuries of the second millennium A.D. a curious change took place in the construction of south Indian temples which even today we cannot fully explain. The vimānas, whose steady growth in size we have been able to follow from Mahaballipuram to Tanjore, shrank beyond recognition, and at the same time the entrance-gates (gopuras) to the temple enclosure gained in importance. This change has been explained by the fact that around the ancient little shrine there steadily grew up, like the annual rings formed on a tree-trunk, new institutions, priests' houses, ancillary shrines and processional streets. Since it was impossible to enlarge the core of the complex, rulers donated magnificent gate-towers in the new sections of the area. This is true of some temple cities, such as Madurai. But there are also examples to the contrary, in which an entire town, complete with a tiny cella and gigantic gopuras, was designed and built in one bout of activity.

South Indian Shivaism developed particularly varied rites for the worship of the vast number of divine manifestations of Shiva. Worship, as taught by adherents of the bhakti school as the way to God, was the centre of religious thinking. New ways were contrived whereby believers could be transported into that frame of mind which was regarded as the prerequisite for cognition of the supreme principle. These innovations are reflected in architecture, in a concept of spatial treatment which no longer had anything in common with the original arrangement, related only to the cult object.

In our discussion of south Indian temples we have already noted that the execution of the interior was neglected; it is therefore all the more surprising that in the inner rings of the temple city, except for the cella, there is hardly any area that is enclosed on all sides. Corridor follows upon corridor; courtyards and so-called 'halls of a thousand pillars' lead to more galleries and streets. The only fixed points visible in this unbroken flow of buildings are the gopuras. Through them alone one reaches one's goal: the smaller the gate, the closer one is to the cella.

Early nāgara style

The north Indian type of temple presumably developed out of an ancient mode of building in bamboo. The Vedic fire sacrifice took place in the open. The superimposition of Dravidian traditions upon Vedic ideas is reflected in the way in which the fire sacrifice was neglected and worship of images came to the fore instead. In order to protect the idols, some of which were modelled in clay and others carved in wood, from the weather, small bamboo tents were built around them. In imitation of bamboo dwellings four bamboo rods were placed in the ground and bent together at the top. The difficult juncture was mastered by bending the soft ends of the bamboo-canes downwards and tying them together within the framework so formed. Vertical plaiting between the rods comprising this framework enclosed the shrine so that it could not be seen from outside. These bamboo shrines were built higher and higher. Cross-bars had

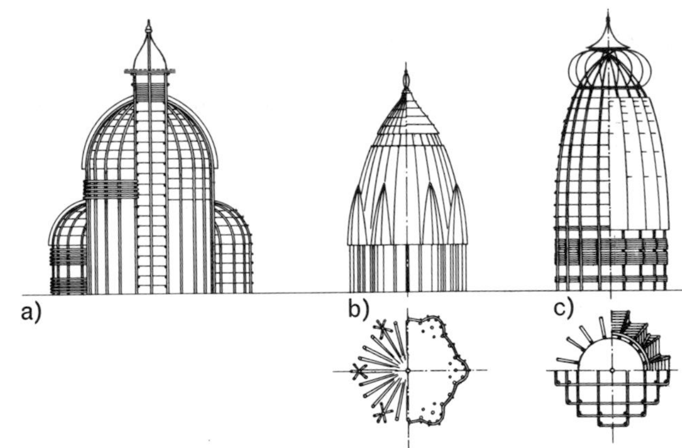

Attempted reconstruction of early bamboo structures
a) Buddhist chaitya-hall
b) and c) bamboo temples in nāgara style

to be inserted to make them stiff enough to resist the wind, and finally pairs of bamboo rods were placed axially in front of the façade and joined to the knot on top. This gave the shrine further stiffening and formed niches on the axes of the structure which could be used to accommodate idols. Lavishly decorated bamboo temples of this kind embellished every town and village in north India. In order to prolong the life of such a temple, wood came to be used instead of bamboo, which quickly rotted.

During the seventh century wood was itself replaced by stone, but the ancient form of the building was retained. Monuments were 'erected' in stone but were not yet 'conceived' in stone.

The spire above the garbha-griha, called 'shikhara', was for static reasons rarely executed in a massive form. Instead the cella is continued in the structure of the shikhara. Above a thin stone cover, which shut off the garbha-griha from view, the chamber tapers, since each course of masonry projects slightly. This false vaulting terminates at the tip of the spire. The early form of the nāgara temple is thus characterized by a cubic sanctuary surrounded by massive walls, over which rises a high spire with a silhouette rather like a parabola, and symmetrically projecting rathas.

Classical nāgara style

Bhuvaneshvar in Orissā and Khajurāho in central India are the two sites where the development of the north Indian type of temple can best be studied. The greatest period at Khajurāho begins about A.D. 950 and lasts for only a century. Early examples of the curved temple tower are found at Bhuvaneshvar, where more than thirty sanctuaries illustrate every step in the continual refinement and differentiation of forms.

This development began in the Chalukya kingdom around Aihole. The imitations in stone of bamboo shrines, which were grafted on to types of building current in this area, inspired Orissan architects. In the middle of the eighth century A.D. they began to erect spires of this kind, called shikhara, as autochthonous 'structive' monuments. For many generations stone towers were roughly parabola-shaped in outline without any other buildings being added to them; only later, at the beginning of the tenth century, was a second architectural body, the 'jagamohan', added to the square spire. The jagamohan corresponds to the mandapa in south India. It will be recalled that originally the dravida temple also stood in the centre of the sanctuary without any additional buildings. In both instances it was not until the second stage of development that the representation of the sacred mountain was associated with an assembly hall in which the faithful were accommodated. The original separation of the two chambers exerted an influence upon the form of all north Indian temples, since when they were cramped together all kinds of structural compromises were required in the transitional zone.

Like the dravida vimāna, the square shikhara, termed rekhā-deul, consists of a cubic base ('bada') and the tower proper ('chapra'). The assembly hall (jagamohan), like the shikhara, has a square ground-plan. Its base is also called a bada, and the terraced roof above it, resulting from the false vaulting, is termed a 'pida'. The tower terminates in a circular plate, upon which rests the 'āmalaka', a fruit-like finial of which the significance is not clear. The rekhā-deul is crowned by the 'kalasha', an imitation of a vase in which rainwater could collect. On a reduced scale this arrangement is repeated upon the roof of the jagamohan; between the pida and the circular terminal plate, here referred to as a 'neck', a massive stone bell is incorporated. One could continue endlessly with the enumeration of the various elements and ornaments.

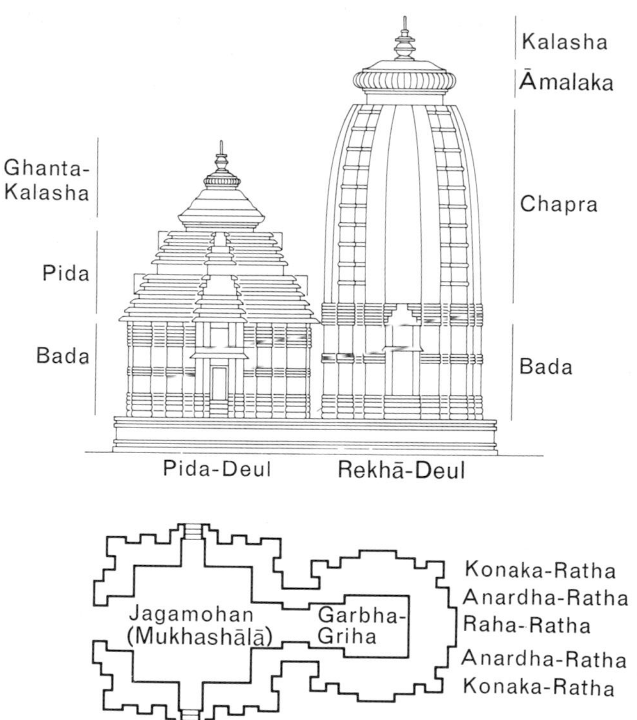

Schematic representation of a nāgara temple

From the eleventh century onward architects occasionally added to the two classical architectural bodies – the cella and assembly hall – two others on the longitudinal axis of the temple. In front of the jagamohan was the 'nat-mandir', or dancing hall, and in front of this a third chamber, the sacrificial hall. All the rooms in the interior have a surprising lack of decoration; the figures and ornaments are concentrated upon the exterior of the building.

We may distinguish between two different principles of composition in the enrichment of the simple tapering shikhara. Most temples at Bhuvaneshvar are 'unipartite', i.e. the basic form is retained however large the shrine is. Small āmalakas divide the tower into several tiers but do not interrupt the soaring line of the parabola. The only significant articulation in this tower comes from the rathas. In order to lend particular emphasis to these wall salients, during the classical phase of the nāgara style architects in most cases added a small recess to introduce the salient. These recesses produce deep shadows and make the rathas appear to stand out more prominently than they really do. The whole exterior is covered with a network of horizontal lines between the storeys and vertical dividing lines between the rathas.

Besides 'unipartite' shikharas there are others with several parts. The 'leit-motif' of such structures is not the net-like rhythm we have just described but the addition of several small shikharas around a main tower. This is a three-dimensional version of a two-dimensional vāstu-purusha mandala. The main tower is the Brahmā-sthāna; around it are grouped, first, fairly large half-shikharas, representing the ring of the 'inner gods', followed by smaller ones representing the rings of the 'outer gods'. The shikhara with several parts originated when the axial niches containing images were no longer continued as 'raha-rathas' as far as the crown of the parabola, but instead were terminated half-way up by a bisected miniature shikhara. This 'konaka-ratha' was then likewise surrounded by a three-quarter shikhara; and finally quarter, half and three-quarter shikharas were arranged on several storeys in such a way as to form heavily articulated zones of miniature buildings, which stretched from the foundations to the main tower and concealed the original simple square plan.

This effect is particularly apparent in the Rājarāni temple. When one walks around it, one has to concentrate in order to be able to reconstruct the geometric form of the building, since from every angle of vision it appears in a different form, as an impenetrable accumulation of rathas and shikharas. One would expect that with a square ground-plan the corners at the diagonals would stand out clearly. But in the Rājarāni temple it is at these very spots that we find recesses, which serve to make the rathas between them project further. This is why it has been repeatedly maintained in scholarly works that here a normal temple tower has simply been co-ordinated diagonally with the jagamohan. This is a misconception, based in part on the fact that the architect of the Rājarāni temple repeated the graduated salients of the façade in the interior, where they have the form of graduated recesses. This at first sight makes it seem as though the ground-plan has been twisted diagonally. This repetition of the ratha motif in the garbha-griha makes the Rājarāni temple one of the few Hindu shrines where one cannot regret the (intentional) discrepancy between the exterior and the interior.

Western buildings, from classical Greece to classicism, are throughout well suited to graphic representation of their façades. An Indian sthapati might speak of an 'architecture of façades' in Europe. The great importance attached to the exterior vertical lines springs from the architects' need to make the monument explicable to the viewer. This is true of the interior as well as the exterior: architects always considered what effect this proportion or that, this treatment of space or that, would have upon those

Ground-plan of the Rājarāni temple at Bhuvaneshvar

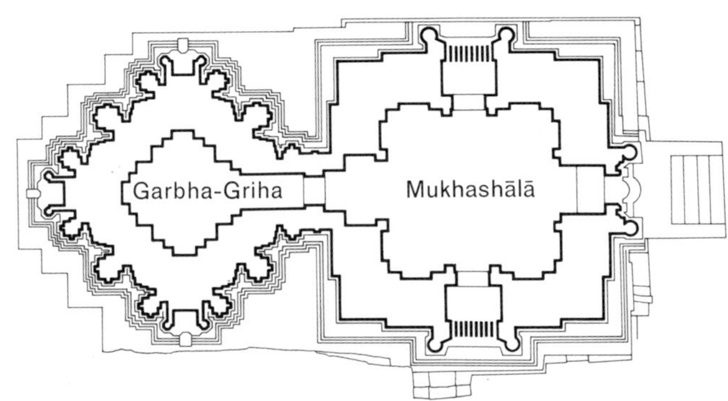

who entered the building. Even the house of God was always adapted to man's view of it. The form or lighting of such elements as domes, barrel-vaulting or colonnades was related solely to the men and women who worshipped in the church. We take this so much for granted that we are inclined to regard it as an architectural axiom – so much so that we occasionally entertain doubts whether a rock-cut temple can really be regarded as architecture, since it has not been 'built'.

Hindu architecture teaches us not to accept some axioms unconditionally. The Orissan temples, for example, have in effect no façades. The vertical sections flow without a break and fuse with the most important of all angles of vision, the view from above. Again, the architectonic system of a temple can best be perceived from an inaccessible viewpoint, namely from the air. The shikhara tapers toward the top, and there are no overlaps or recesses even in the lower part. Thus there would be no better vantage-point from which to view the monument as comprehensively as possible than a point directly above the temple, exactly on its vertical axis. From this perspective all the ornaments which, to those viewing the temple from other angles, appear to be swelling luxuriantly in ever more exaggerated forms, would fall into place as subordinate to a geometric order; this order is only imperfectly reflected in the ground-plan of such buildings, because a ground-plan is after all only an arbitrarily drawn horizontal section. The north Indian temple tower, as an image of the cosmic order, has every side facing outwards into space.

The cosmic axis appears in the lingam and on the outside of the temple is visible in the circular 'neck stone' and also in the kalasha, where the manifested and non-manifested worlds meet. Absolute symmetry and axiality are a theological 'sine qua non' of the building and not the mere product of aesthetic fashions.

The slight extent to which the builders of north Indian temples were concerned to achieve a certain spatial effect is evident from the fact that we are consistently disappointed whenever we seek a sense of space in a jagamohan or a garbha-griha. The proportions are fixed by a geometric and symbolic order. The architect had no opportunity to realize any concepts of space other than those implicit in the proportions laid down. The question of a 'spatial effect' is in fact irrelevant, since the monument was not designed with man in mind, but instead is a record in stone of the priests' mystical visions of how God might manifest himself in architectural form.

Konārak

In the middle of the thirteenth century near the sacred city of Bhuvaneshvar work began on the last gigantic temple to be constructed in nāgara style. Built in honour of the sun god Sūrya, it was a shikhara some 75 metres high; with its jagamohan in front, it was to represent the celestial chariot in which the sun god journeys daily across the firmament. Twelve gigantic stone wheels decorate the socle and seven pairs of horses draw the monument (strangely enough, towards the east). The realization of such a vast temple was, however, beyond the technical possibilities of that era. Even before the tower was completed the foundations subsided into the soft sand of the dunes. The shikhara collapsed and only the jagamohan remained intact. In the nineteenth century its walls, too, seemed likely to cave in, since in buildings of such monumental dimensions corbel-vaulting is no longer safe. The British authorities therefore had to fill in the interior with supports and to wall up the accesses. There is thus no longer any opportunity to see this largest of all interiors in Hindu architecture. It differed from the assembly halls at Bhuvaneshvar in so far as four massive pillars were placed in the chamber, the architraves of which supported the corbel-vaulting (see plan, p. 172).

In front of the jagamohan was the nat-mandir, the dancing pavilion. Its pyramid-shaped roof has been destroyed, but the finest elements – the pillars covered in reliefs and a base treated no less lavishly – are preserved in excellent condition. Besides geometric ornaments and miniature buildings, we encounter time and again the motif of 'apsaras', celestial nymphs, or of 'devadāsī', temple dancing girls and musicians. These embellish both the dancing pavilion and the bases of the jagamohan and shikhara. Here, however, they alternate with 'mithuna' couples, rendered with imagination and verve either on medallions or on the spokes of wheels, sometimes larger than life-size; they have been referred to as merely obscene by some art historians incapable of appreciating such an erotic spectacle. To what extent these were connected with Tantric rites we cannot consider here. It is, however, certain that the adherents of the Tantric rite regarded their customs as dangerous to non-initiates. They built the Konārak temple at a very lonely spot in the sand dunes on the coast of the Bay of Bengal.

Khajurāho

The temples at Khajurāho likewise bear the imprint of the Tantric rite; however, they were built not in a lonely place but in the capital of the Chandella kingdom. Within a short space of time – exactly one century – the simple 'uni-partite' shikhara here developed into a complex geometric form consisting of several parts. The Kandāriya Mahādeo temple exemplifies the final stage.

In the late temples at Khajurāho the typical north Indian ground-plan is modified. Inside the tower there is a pradakshinā-patha around the garbha-griha. It was lit by three verandahs situated at the cardinal points. As at Konārak, the architect felt that the 'mahā-mandapa' was too large to be covered by simple corbel-vaulting. The corbelled courses of the roof were only taken as far as the squares of the columns and a new corbel-vaulting begins above the architraves of this colonnade.

Only the garbha-griha containing the lingam is devoid of decoration. But the interior circumambulatory path and the mahā-mandapa with its verandahs in front (called artha-mandapas) are seen by the Khajurāho architect as parts of the exterior. The profiles of their bases and corbel-vaulting are just as

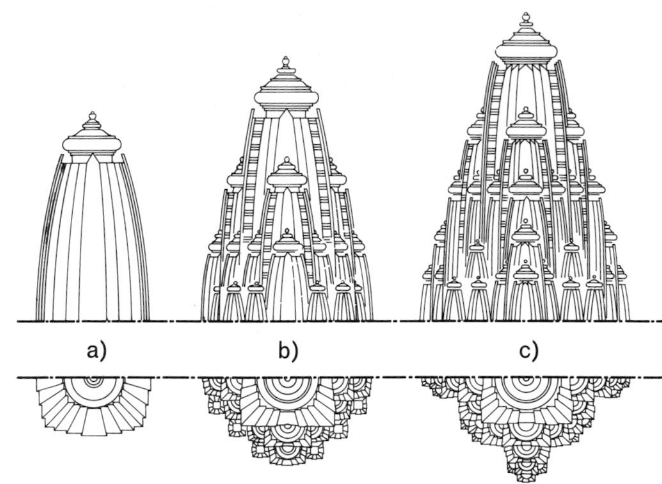

The development from the 'unipartite' to the 'multipartite' shikhara tower at Khajurāho
a) Adinatha temple, Jain, A.D. 950
b) Paraswanatha temple, Jain, A.D. 970
c) Kandāriya Mahādeo temple, Hindu, A.D. 1050

extravagantly treated, down to the tiniest details, as the outer 'skin' of the building. It is probably no coincidence that the interior, as well as being decorated, is generously lit, because only in the clear light of the tropical sun could the gradations and the lavish sculpture produce their effect; in the interior of a dim temple they would be scarcely noticeable.

Regional developments

Somnāthpur

In the thirteenth century, while the north Indian architectural tradition was approaching its apogee, the Hoysala family in the so-called 'later Chalukya kingdom' built some temples whose style is a fusion of elements of dravida and nāgara; it is usually termed 'vesara' style. The three most important sanctuaries of this type are those of Belūr, Halebīd and Somnāthpur; of these the Keshava temple at Somnāthpur is the best preserved. Here again we find the Buddhist scheme of ground-plan, which was later adopted in dravida temples: a court surrounded by cells, originally with a stūpa or a Hindu tower temple in the middle. The temple of Somnāthpur, however, has three cellas or three towers, dedicated to various manifestations of Vishnu. The most important of these, the Keshava, is venerated in the middle cella.

We shall now discuss this small shrine in rather more detail, since in it we can observe especially distinctly the Hindu sthapati's fondness for geometric constructions. Each cella is star-shaped in outline, and the platform on which the cella rests is also star-shaped. This is not just a whim of the architect, but a further development of a geometric form with which we are already familiar from the roof structure of the Hellenistic tomb at Mylasa, east of Miletus, dating from the second century B.C. The vaulting of this mausoleum was achieved by placing stone beams diagonally upon a square of architraves, as an inscribed square. Next shorter stone beams were laid, also as an inscribed square, and so on until the ever-diminishing opening could be covered by a slab. The basic form of this so-called lantern ceiling presumably originates from Asia Minor.

The cells around the temple at Somnāthpur have lantern ceilings. The inscribed square also appears in the ground-plan of the three shrines. The star-shaped form of the platform and of the exterior outline is brought about in each case by turning one square by 22° 30′.

In the same way as we reconstructed the geometric structure of an ancillary shrine of the Brahmeshvara temple, let us now follow the various steps that led to the ground-plan of the Keshava temple. We shall see that the form of the sanctuaries and also of the entire temple were determined by inscribed squares and squares turned within circumscribed circles.

After the cardinal points had been established, the centre and the main axes of the temple were fixed and the 'square of the earth' laid out, in the dimensions of the prospective sanctuary. In this basic square, indicated in our diagram by S_0, three progressively smaller squares were inscribed: S_1, S_2, and S_3. These squares were then turned by 45° within the circles (C_1, C_2, and C_3) which circumscribe them. This produces the squares S'_1, S'_2 and S'_3. Around the points where the square S'_3 intersects with the main south, west and north axes, which we shall call P_s, P_w and P_n, circles were drawn, to which S_2 and S'_2 are tangents. In these circles the star-shaped sanctuaries and platforms rotate. S'_2, moreover, encircles the ground-plan of the temple, and S_2, if its sides are extended, enables the basic square to be divided into 16 panels.

The Keshava temple at Somnāthpur. The evolution of a ground-plan from the circle and square

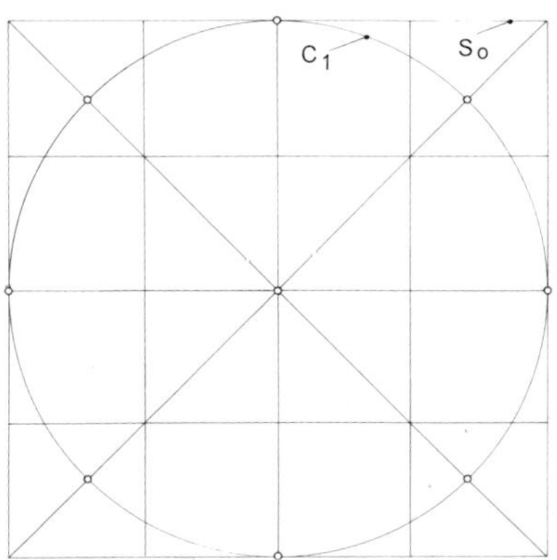

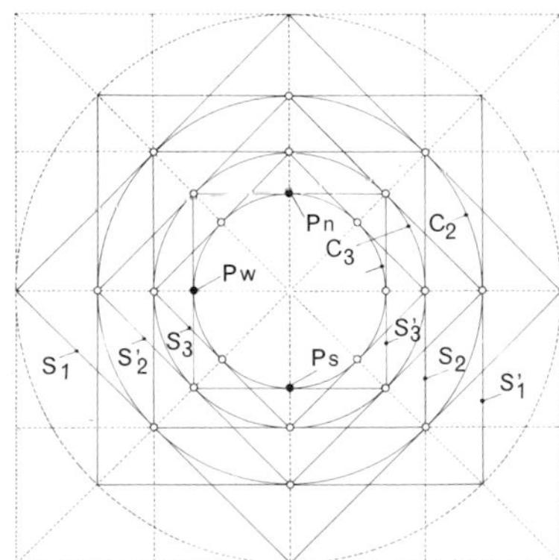

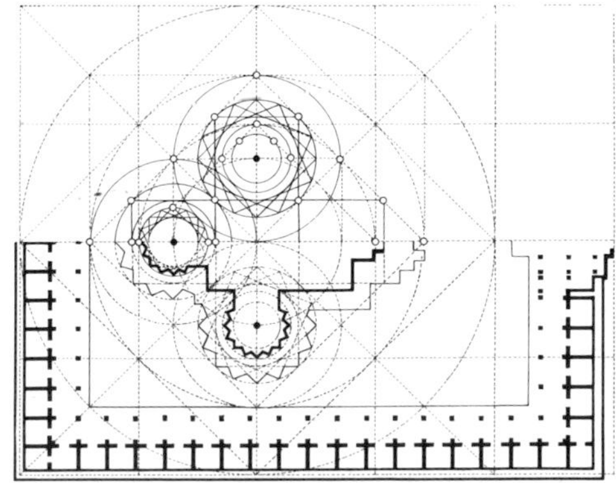

The size of the recessed temple court is fixed by S_1.

In each panel of the plan along the outer border provision was made for four cells. This makes sixteen cells on each side of the basic square. The temple court was enlarged toward the east in order to make room for larger groups of pilgrims and to provide those entering the court with a general view of the whole temple. Since along the longitudinal side of the court there are 20 cells instead of 16, one may infer that the layout was simply enlarged by the width of one panel. But astonishingly enough the proportion of 4:5 panels is not adhered to exactly. The cells along the longitudinal sides were somewhat compressed, yielding a ratio of 4:4.9. Although this cannot be attributed to an error in measurement by the artisans, since otherwise the work has been carried out with meticulous precision, we may assume that originally provision was made in the plan for an enlargement by exactly one panel width. At least the number of cells is in the ratio 4:5.

The vertical articulation of the three star-shaped shrines is continued from the base to the tops of the towers. In this respect the temple resembles the north Indian shikharas. The south Indian motif of horizontal stratification is brought to mind by the pronounced horizontal profiles of all the architectural elements. The term vesara for this hybrid style has been much discussed in recent decades, since the various medieval texts seem to contradict one another. In some of them a vesara is a geographical term for the country between the Vindhya mountains and the river Krishna; in others it is employed to denote a circular temple. But since there are virtually no circular temples in India, it is clear that in the ancient texts a building was meant which is defined in a striking way by the circle. This is true of the temple at Somnāthpur and several sanctuaries in the neighbourhood, so that one definition of the term vesara need not exclude the other.

Mount Ābū

At the beginning of the second millennium A.D. the west coast of India was ruled by the Solankī dynasty of Gujarat. One of these kings' ministers, Vimala Sah (Shah), in his capacity as commander of the army, was sent to the town of Chandravati to pacify a rebellious principality. After he had carried out his mission he asked a Jain monk how he could do penance for the bloodshed he had caused. Deliberate homicide was not expiable, the monk informed him, but if he felt the necessity to do a good deed, then he should give a donation for Ābū, a sacred place of pilgrimage situated close to the town.

Vimala Sah had a sanctuary built in white marble which in its ground-plan and vertical section heralds essential features of the Keshava temple at Somnāthpur. (For plan of Ābū, see p. 134, of Somnāthpur p. 133.) The temple stands in a court, surrounded by a double colonnade and a circle of cells. The so-called 'gudha-mandapa' at Ābū corresponds to the central mandapa of the Keshava temple. The garbha-griha adjoins it on the west side, whereas at Somnāthpur it is separated from the mandapa by a small vestibule. On the south and north sides the porches of the gudha-mandapa project far forward, giving the ground-plan the form of a cross. In front of the gudha-mandapa is a small columnar hall, the 'nav-choki'. The most interesting room of the entire complex, the dancing hall, called 'ranga-mandapa', was only added one hundred years after the temple had been completed. A wide room, without any intervening supports, was needed for the ritual dances; a high shikhara roof was out of the question since the columns would not bear a heavy weight. The way in which the corbelled dome was constructed will be discussed in Chapter V.

Two hundred years after work had commenced on Vimala's temple, the brothers Tejapāla and Vastupala, also ministers in the service of the Solankī dynasty, erected another temple with the same ground-plan next to that of Vimala. They planned a dancing pavilion from the start and gave greater emphasis to the cruciform ground-plan. From this it was only a small step to the transformation of the porches of the gudha-mandapa into two more shrines containing images, which would give the same ground-plan as in Somnāthpur.

Plates

Bhuvaneshvar

155 The Brahmeshvara temple, dating from the 11th century, seen from the east. In the centre is the assembly hall and behind it the tower above the sanctum. The pyramid-shaped roof of the square assembly hall has terraced courses of stone slabs with accentuated horizontal articulation, like those on south Indian temple towers.

156 The Brahmeshvara temple, seen from the south-east.

157 Profile of socle of the cella of the Brahmeshvara temple.

158 a) Window of the Mukteshvara temple, worked monolithically. The assembly hall of a north Indian temple is usually lit by a single window such as this.

158 b) In front of the entrance to the assembly hall of the Mukteshvara temple is a stone gateway with a round arch. Remembering the Indian saying, 'The (true) arch does not rest', the sthapatis (priest-architects) hardly ever built with radially cut stone slabs, but instead set one slab horizontally upon another; the round arch is thus very rare in Hindu architecture.

158 c) A niche for an image on the south side of the Mukteshvara temple. The formal canon has been adopted from architecture in wood.

159 The Rājarāni temple, dating from the 12th–13th centuries A.D. Note the refinement and differentiation of the architectonic temple form and of the detail, typical of the last period of greatness in the history of the sacred city of Bhuvaneshvar.

160 On approaching the temple one sees that each form is resolved into proportionately smaller ones, so that the viewer is presented with a new play of forms at whatever distance he stands from the monument.

161 Even if one approaches to within a few inches of the temple wall, new details emerge.

Caurasi

162 The shikhara of the Vārāhī temple, from the 12th century A.D., seen from the west. This small shrine, the form of which was determined by the requirements of the Tantric rite, merits particular attention, since the significance of its proportions and imagery is elucidated in the 'Shilpa-prakāsha', a medieval manuscript written on palm-leaves. Because the temple is dedicated to a female deity, the tower, i.e. the cella, has a rectangular ground-plan instead of the usual square one.

163 In this nameless dilapidated shrine at Bhuvaneshvar one can see the pyramidal shape of the vaulting, the interior having been exposed to the daylight.

Konārak

164 Steps leading into the dancing pavilion of the Sūrya temple, dating from the 13th century A.D.

165 The assembly hall, seen from the dancing pavilion. Behind it towers up the highest of all Indian shikharas.

166 Innumerable bands in relief, featuring dancing girls and musicians, cover the base of the dancing pavilion. This detail of an incomplete section shows the method of working.

167 Detail of a completed section of the same wall.

168 The geometric system of the Sūrya temple and its ancillary shrines has not yet been fully established, since we lack accurate photographs of the building. The countless salients and recesses of the socle profile present a confusing picture.

169 Twelve stone wheels were incorporated in the socle zone of the Sūrya temple, set between mithuna couples and apsaras. The temple was visualized as the chariot of the sun god, rolling across the firmament.

170 Small medallions in the spokes of the wheels are filled with fanciful representations of mithuna couples.

The Brahmeshvara temple at Bhuvaneshvar
Ground-plan, sections and elevations 1:300

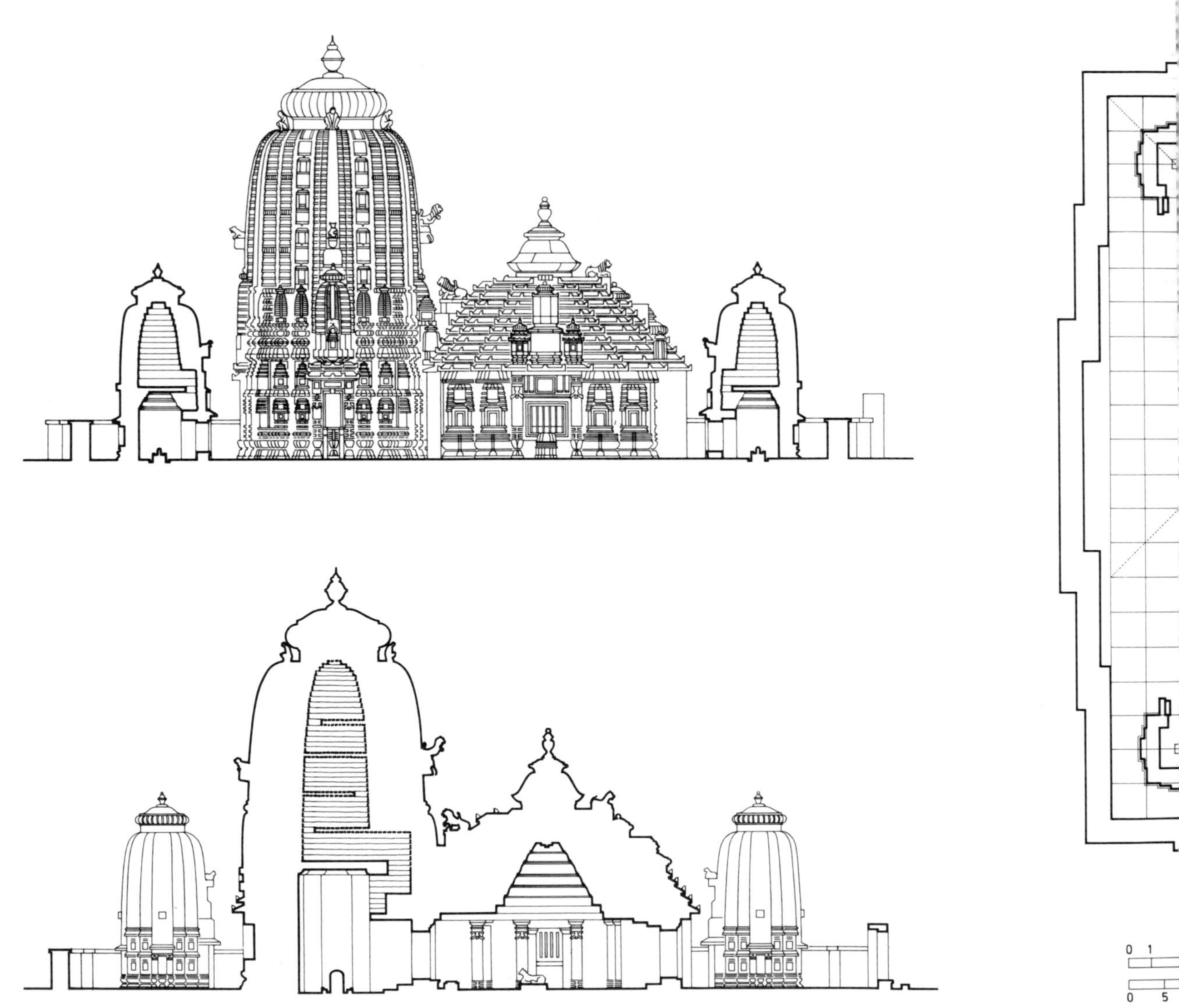

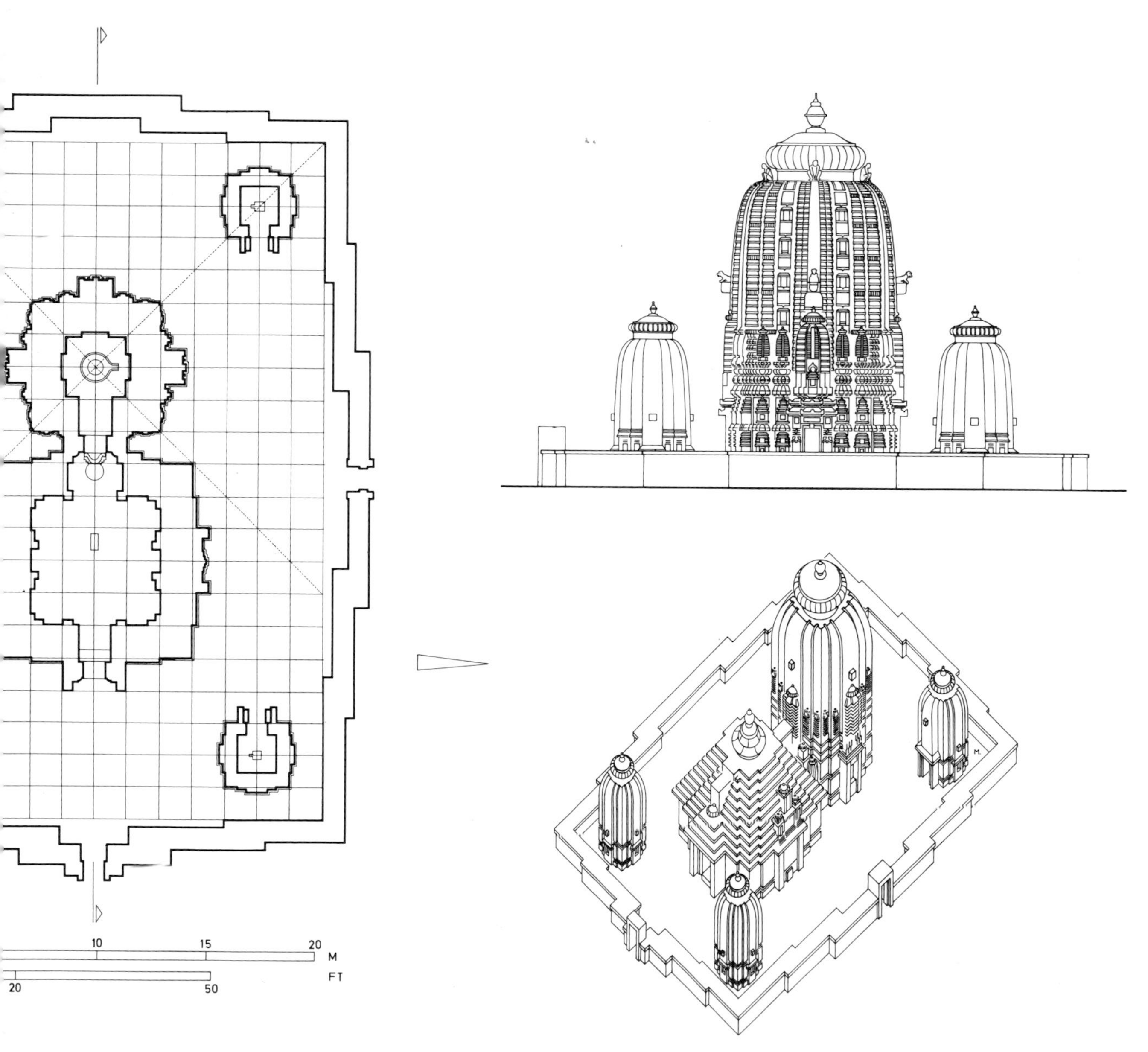
10
15
20
M
FT
20
50
M.

Notes

Bhuvaneshvar

Here more than one hundred temples have survived from the period between the eighth and thirteenth centuries A.D., most of which, however, are no longer in use. Even from a distance as one approaches the city one can see the tall curved outline of a shikhara, some 45 metres high, towering up over the palm-trees. It is the tower over the cella of the Lingarāja temple, dating from the twelfth century. All around the main temple are about seventy to eighty shrines, dedicated to various gods, which were built at different times. The sacred compound and the Lingarāja ('king of phalli') may be entered only by Hindus; the temple custodians keep guard at the gate in the high enclosure wall. We therefore have to concern ourselves with several of the smaller sanctuaries, which are, however, no less important.

As building material a light-coloured sandstone was used, obtained from the quarries at Udayajiri, about seven kilometres from the city. Only the foundations and enclosure walls are built in part of the crude, dark red laterite that was quarried at the site. Several temples that had previously collapsed were faithfully reconstructed by the Archaeological Survey of India, using the ancient building methods: first the structural work on the tower was carried out, in polished squared ashlar without any joints; then followed the elaboration of the exterior and finally of the interior.

Caurasi

In medieval architectural manuals all conceivable variants of the north Indian type of temple are discussed in detail. One of these variants, called 'khakara', is rectangular in plan and is reserved for the female manifestation of Shiva. The Vārāhī temple at Caurasi is a typical khakara temple. Although it has been in use without a break since it was built in the twelfth century, it only came to the notice of historians of Indian architecture a few decades ago. Caurasi is a remote village, not recorded on any map of Orissā, and known only to the inhabitants of the immediate vicinity. With the aid of a recently discovered manuscript, the 'Shilpa-prakāsha', it could be proved from this temple that most of the Tantric reliefs were composed on the basis of a geometric magic symbol (yantram). The representations in relief, whether they were of mythical beasts or mithuna couples, were intended to divert the attention of non-initiates away from the geometric image, which was of far greater importance. Only the initiates, who could identify the symbol in the reliefs, were to enjoy the opportunity to draw magic power from the yantram. It is tempting to assume that a link could be established between works of sculpture and the Tantric yantram wherever this sectarian doctrine was professed. It has not yet been possible to examine closely the effects which Tantrism exerted upon Hindu architecture and sculpture, since the Tantric communities that still exist today do not reveal their secret doctrines to outsiders and keep their ancient manuals in their temples.

Konārak

A description of this sanctuary, dedicated to the sun, has survived from the sixteenth century. Abu-'l-Fazl, the court historian of Emperor Akbar, writes in his journal about the Sūrya temple: 'Not far from Purī there is a temple dedicated to the sun. The total public revenue collected over twelve years was spent on building it ... The walls are some 150 hands high and 19 hands thick ... If one approaches the temple by one of the nine flights of steps, one sees a spacious hall and a large adjacent room, all built of stone, in which the sun and the other planets are carved. All around the temple human figures are represented in various 'versions', some standing on their heads, others upright, seated or reclining, and others again full of wisdom. In addition one sees various kinds of female musicians and a row of strange animals which must have sprung from the imagination. It is said here that more than 700 years ago a certain king, Rāja Narasingh Deva, completed this great monument for his own glory. In the neighbourhood are some further 28 temples, six of them opposite the entrance gates and 22 outside the sacred compound. Around each of them legends have accumulated.' This account shows that in the opinion of the local inhabitants the temple was built as early as the ninth century A.D. But all the stylistic features suggest that it was not erected until the thirteenth century A.D.

The Vārāhī temple at Caurasi
Ground-plan and vertical sections 1:150

A Garbha-griha
B Mukhashālā

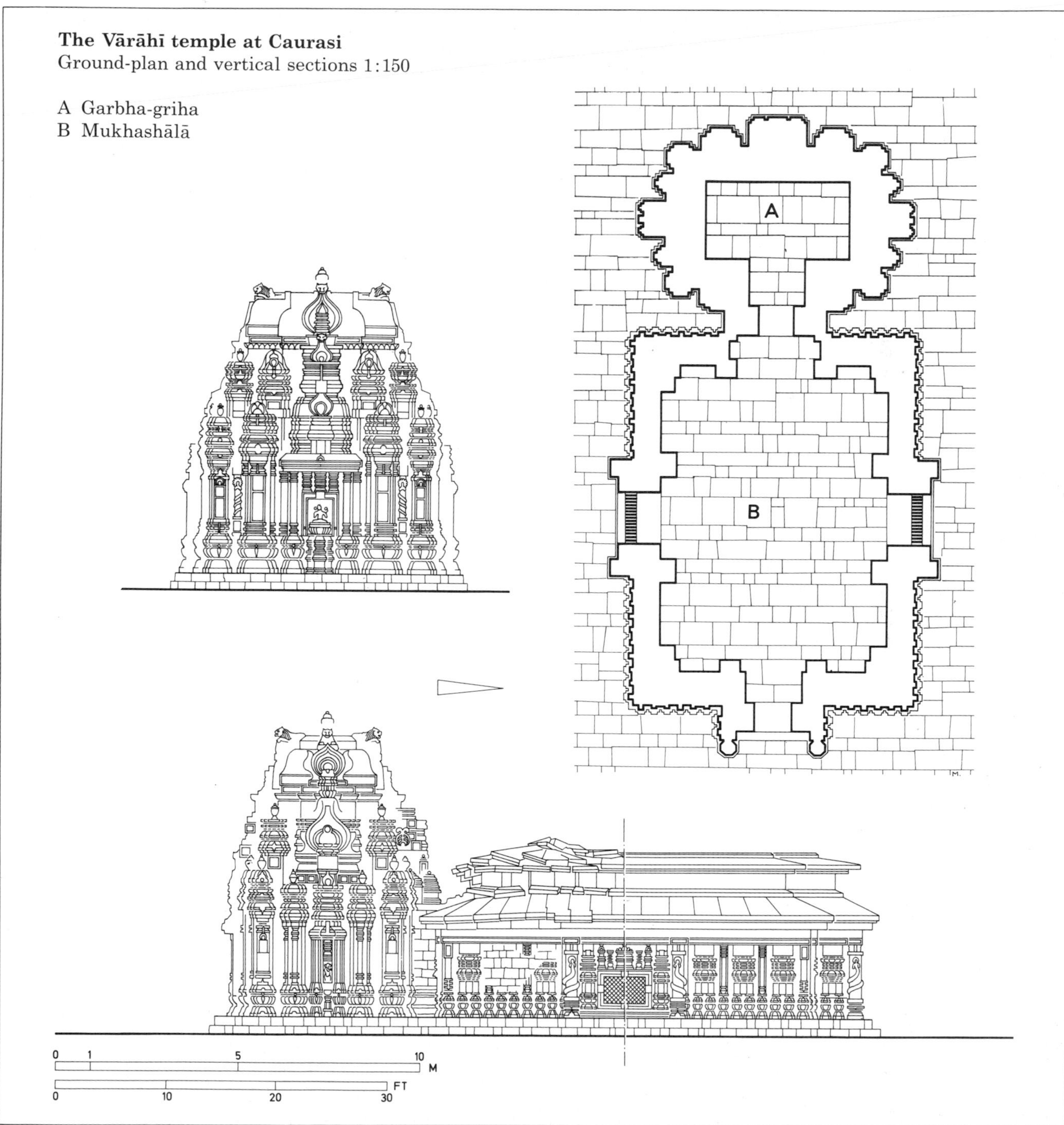

The Sūrya temple at Konārak

Ground-plan of the jagamohan and garbha-griha; elevation and vertical section of the jagamohan 1:800

A Garbha-griha
B Jagamohan

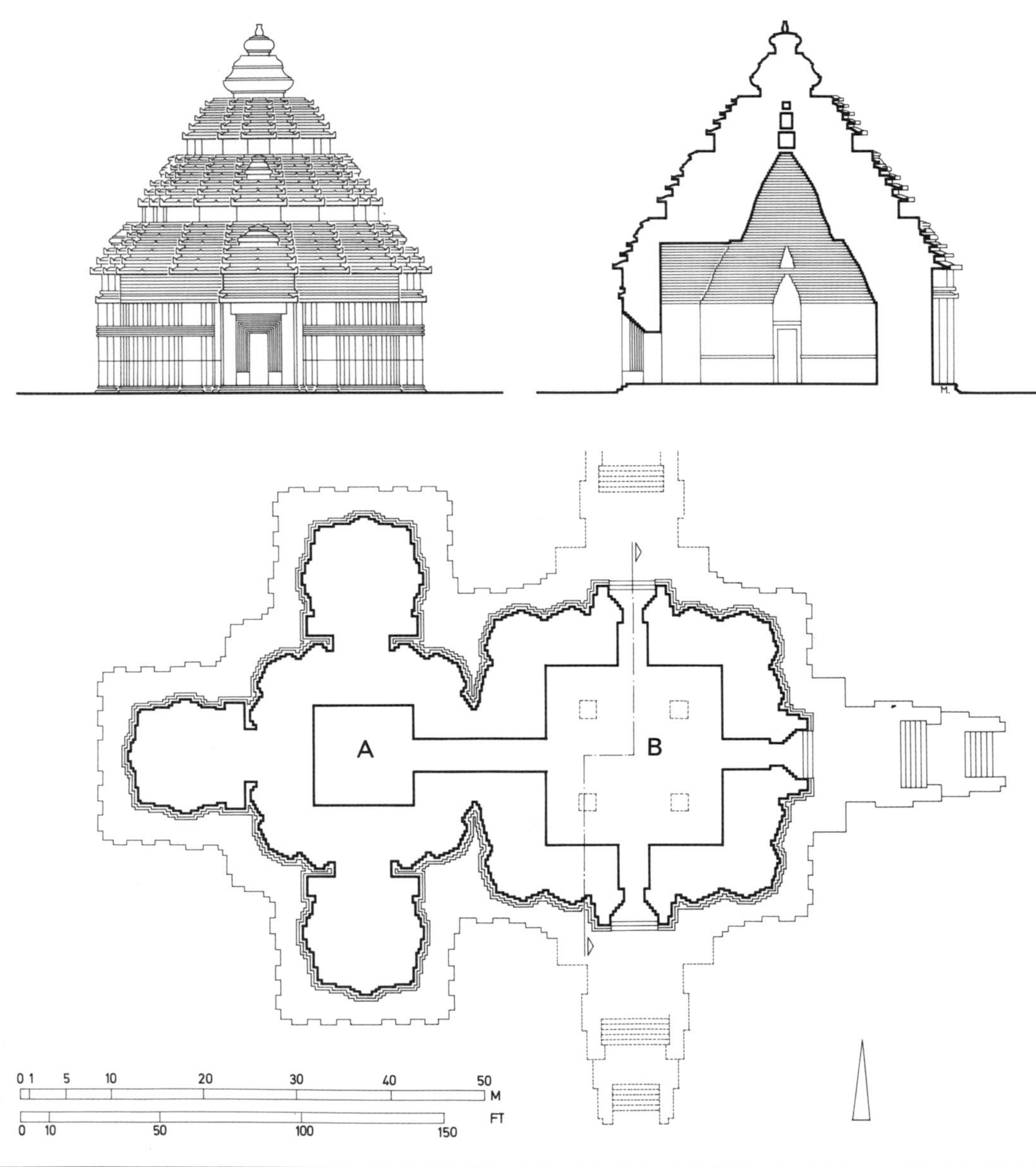

5. Materials and Construction Methods

The Indian sthapati was primarily magician, astrologer, and expert in geometry. In a world which from the beginning of the kali yuga had been filled with misery and chaos, he sought to create in microcosm an image of the law-governed macrocosm. During the Gupta period it was still his chief task to produce a simple stone shelter for the divine image. As soon as he felt himself equal to this technical task, he turned towards the more esoteric aspects of building a sanctuary. The temple as cosmic mountain, or as cave, or as an efficacious magic diagram, or as garbha-griha (womb), ensuring procreation and fertility: these were the ideas which now moved him, and which led to a variety of forms, to architecture of geometric austerity, and to the elaboration of the most complex rites.

Most manuals on architecture are therefore collections of rules designed to facilitate the translation of a theological concept into plastic form. Each step which the architect takes is regarded from the angle of ritual purity and magic effect, only rarely from the angle of structural expediency. Only in this way can one understand why even during the greatest period of temple-building use was made of simple methods of construction, such as in other cultures were characteristic solely of the initial stages of architectural design.

Materials

In the 'Mayamata' manuscript we read the following: 'Stone or wood is worthy of gods, Brahmins, kings and hermits, but unsuited to Vaishyas and Shūdras.' Thus the material used was linked to the caste system. Other manuals do allow the use of stone as a material for all temples, irrespective of whether they were constructed by a Brahmin or a Shūdra; but the caste of the builder still had to be expressed by the colour of the stone. White stone was to be used only by Brahmins, red by Kshatriyas, yellow by Vaishyas and black by Shūdras. The colours of the cosmic mountain Meru, mentioned in Chapter II, determine this attribution. The rules on the colour of the building material do not refer exclusively to stone; should it be decided to build in brick, here too the basic material, in this case clay, must have exactly the prescribed colour.

Materials are not only co-ordinated with caste but also with sex. A temple in stone and brick is termed male, one of brick and wood female. If all three materials were combined, the temple was considered neuter. As soon as the building materials had been taken from their natural environment, they were freed from all former associations by the performance of certain rites. The felling of the tree, the baking of the brick, or the quarrying of the stone initiated the process whereby the material was transubstantiated from its mundane state to 'corpus dei', as the temple was regarded.

It is known that as early as Vedic times there was a rite whereby brick was transubstantiated by baking it. From the sixth century A.D. onward stone is regarded as equivalent to brick as a building material. It, too, undergoes a transformation of its substance. In subsequent centuries stone seems to oust brick completely, so that finally we read in medieval manuals: 'It is 100 times more meritorious to found a temple in brick than one in wood with a thatched roof; and it is even 10,000 times more meritorious to found a temple in stone than one in brick.'

North Indian temples are distinguished by the uniformity of the material used. In classical times they were built exclusively in stone. In south India, on the other hand, architects preferred to combine various materials in order to make the best use of the qualities specific to each. Since most temples were covered with a thin layer of white stucco, the change of material did not offend the eye.

The process of manufacturing brick was equated with the sacrificial rite in which the believer making the sacrifice modelled a body in clay and transubstantiated it with the aid of fire. By this act each brick was given an individual spiritual aspect as well as its material one. For this reason the Indian sthapati found it reprehensible to re-use the bricks of a ruined temple in different circumstances. Material which had already been given its identity on a previous occasion could only be efficacious in this original context. The manufacture of bricks was carried out only under certain astrological conditions, which varied according to the purpose for which the bricks were to be used. Since the manufacture of new bricks would naturally take place under a different constellation from that prevailing when the bricks in a ruined building had been made, this in itself was sufficient reason to prevent the latter from being re-used.

Sages therefore repeatedly warned their disciples that they should only employ new material made expressly for the building they were immediately concerned with, for otherwise impurities would enter and great suffering would result. These rules relate both to wood and stone. The process of transforming the nature of wood began first in the forest. At an exactly calculated hour the priest-architects and astrologers would accompany the wood-cutters to the trees that had been selected. In the same way as they had called on the earth spirits to leave the future building site, so that it should belong to God alone, they now exorcized the spirits from the tree: 'Let goblins, spirits and demons retreat, O tree. May Suma, the moon, henceforth afford thee strength. To ye, sons of the earth, gods and gnomes, good fortune. I am about to carry out this task, so pray be so good as to change your abode' or: 'O tree, go into the temple for the benefit of all the arboreal realms. There shalt thou be in safety from fire and from the woodcutter's axe. Thou shalt occupy the position of a god and the people will worship thee.'

The veneration of the wood originates from the ancient metaphor of the tree as cosmos, of the trunk as the axis of the cosmos and the branches as the rotating universe.

The arch

In the cities of the Indus valley civilization it was a common practice to span a wide aperture in a wall by a corbelled arch. The Indians kept to this mode of construction until the Muslim invasion. Even under Islamic rule Hindu artisans constructed arches in Muslim buildings by corbelling, since they were loath to abandon a three-thousand-year tradition. The method is very simple: the stones or bricks in each course jut out a little further into the opening of the door or window, making the gap progressively smaller until it can be covered with a single stone or brick.

Small spans were covered with a single lintel. In large medieval sanctuaries there are also many long lintels, which however are relieved by a corbelled arch placed above them, so that in fact they only support the stone filling in the triangular aperture between the lintel and the corbelled arch.

Most early civilizations are familiar with the corbelled arch. As an example we may mention the Lion Gate at Mycenae. The Aegean architects resorted to exactly the same corbelled constructions at the very same time as the builders of Harappā and Mohenjo-daro perceived in them a safe and economical way of spanning monumental gates and window apertures.

'An arch never rests.' This ancient Indian saying is always cited when it is a matter of justifying this relatively primitive corbelled construction. This explanation, which in the last resort is a theological one, seems convincing in view of the fact that whenever any action is taken in India its mystical connotations are accorded considerable prominence. And yet the sthapati's lack of interest in the structural appearance of a building seems to be primarily responsible for this conscious adoption of traditional primitive structures. Corbelling is especially striking when it is employed to make a semicircular form, e.g. an arch. In front of the Mukteshvara temple at Bhuvaneshvar, for example, there is a massive gate with a round arch, in which the divine image was swung to and fro during the performance of certain rites. This stone arch does not have the cusped shape common in corbelled constructions. Its contour and lavish ornaments follow exactly the curve of the arch. This may seem to us a violation of the corbelled arch principle; stones cut radially would conform better to our concept of an arch. But the sthapati preferred a horizontal arrangement of courses running through all the architectural elements, and he saw no need to deviate from this principle for formal reasons.

The true arch was known in at least some regions of India. We find it set in ashlar masonry on the Bhitragon temple (fifth century A.D.) and composed of shaped bricks on the Bodh Gayā temple (seventh century A.D.). Since these are the only two examples preserved from three thousand years of building prior to the coming of Islam, we may conclude that the sthapatis were never really conscious of the true arch. The two arches on the Indian sub-continent that have stones cut radially presumably owe their existence to foreign influence. They may even have been erected by Persian or Greek architects.

Vaulting

By projecting the corbelled arch into the third dimension one obtains barrel-shaped corbel vaulting. Since only the lower parts of the houses at Mohenjo-daro have survived, we cannot judge whether as early as the Indus valley civilization larger spans were covered in this way. A preliminary stage in the development of vaulting is to be found in the drainage system of these towns. The conduits, which are rectangular in cross-section, are built of brick. They are located in the middle of the street, directly beneath the paving, and are covered by removable flag stones. The upper layers of the brickwork were made to jut out, so that a cap-stone of smaller width could be used.

This early example of a corbelled construction leads us right into the heart of the problem of how corbelled arches or vaults had to be constructed if they were not to collapse. A calculation involving a knowledge of statics was, of course, out of the question for these ancient master craftsmen. They relied upon the experience of their forefathers and regarded the construction of each temple as a new venture, a new experiment.

If the coping-stone of a wall is allowed to project, as

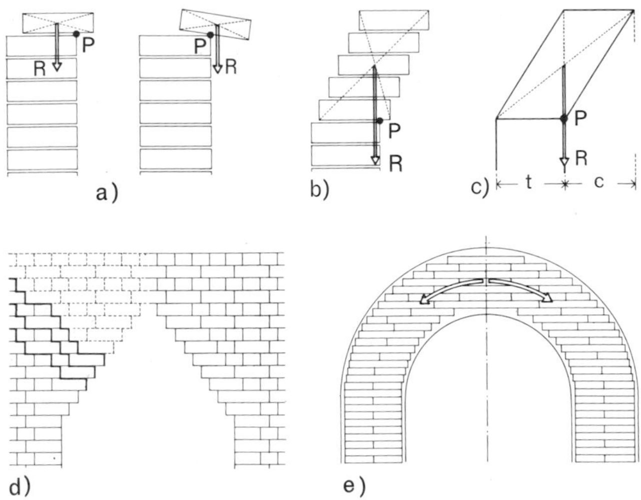

Behaviour of various corbel constructions according to the laws of statics

in Fig. a, the stone will topple over from its own weight unless its centre of gravity rests within the limits of the wall. Correspondingly, when several projecting stones are superimposed on one another, their centre of gravity must also be within these same limits, i.e. to the left of the pivot (P), as shown in our diagram b. This requirement is met by the projecting courses of the sewers at Mohenjo-daro. Diagram c shows that projections can only be constructed in this way when the width of the corbel (c) is smaller than the width of the stone, i.e. the thickness of the wall (w). If c = w, the resultant will run through P; even a slight shift can upset the equilibrium and the stone will fall. If the projections are to jut out even further, the stones at the rear must be so heavily weighted or firmly anchored that the equilibrium is restored. In the case of door and window apertures, this weighting is provided by the masonry above and to the side of the corbelled arch. Without this weighting the arch would collapse. When the arch was being built, there was as yet nothing in the structure to provide such weighting, and for this purpose centring or temporary framing had to be used, unless one took care to ensure that each stone in the arch was set with a weight on its rear part, as illustrated in Fig. d.

The earliest extant example of corbelled barrel-vaulting is in the chaitya-hall at Chezarla, which we have already discussed. As may be seen from diagram 'c', the brick courses jutting out along both longitudinal walls could be piled up without any risk until the width of the corbelling approached the thickness of the wall. Since the clear width of the interior was larger than two thicknesses of wall, the central part of the barrel-vaulting could be completed only with the aid of centring. The vaulting, as in the Roman true vault, only acquired stability when the coping-stones were laid. The two 'arms' of the vault lean towards each other. When they are projected further and meet, they form a barrel-vault which can withstand the pressure; the same horizontal thrusts appear as in Roman barrel-vaulting (Fig. e). Indian architects had a predilection for corbel-vaulting because they had a fixed notion that in this kind of construction only vertical forces made themselves felt. But this is only true so long as $c < w$. But in most cases $w > c$, so that the so-called corbel vaults often look like Roman vaulting, the only difference being that the joints in Indian vaulting are less favourably positioned than they are in the case of Roman vaulting.

The north Indian temple consists of a garbha-griha and a mukhashālā; both as a rule are square in ground-plan and have corbel-vaulting. In the shikhara the cavity above the cella narrows towards the top in a curve rather similar to the exterior outline of the tower. It seems to be no coincidence that the cella is often as wide as two wall thicknesses. This proportion is fixed on one hand by the vāstu-purusha mandala and on the other, no doubt, by the sthapatis' experience that a pure corbel construction could only be carried to this extent (see, for example, the Brahmeshvara temple at Bhuvaneshvar).

In the mukhashālā the relationship of clear width and wall thickness is less favourable. Attempts were made to obtain the necessary equilibrium by widening the roof. By doing this the resultant is moved to the pivot (P). If it is still located outside the limits of the masonry, the last stone slabs are set with the aid of centring and the coping-stone transforms the structure, which juts out on all sides, into a pyramid-shaped cross-vault. The horizontal thrust which makes itself felt must be absorbed by the friction resistance of the horizontal joints.

The architects of the Jain temple at Mount Ābū reached the limits of what was statically possible in the corbelling of the courses of the low domes above the dancing pavilion. The vaulting, with tiers of concentric rings, supported only by columns, rises above an octagon consisting of architraves. Now that we have examined the statics of other corbelled structures, it is no longer necessary to explain that here the most varied factors have to act together to prevent the dome collapsing. Such a dome would not be conceivable as a pure corbelled construction with the lines of force running exclusively in a vertical direction. The easiest solution would have been to use clamps to anchor the slabs of each ring together. If this had been done, the horizontal thrust could have been absorbed without difficulty. Since the temples at Mount Ābū are still in use, it has not yet been possible to verify whether clamps were in fact used. In the opinion of some experts the builders of these relatively primitive structures were probably unfamiliar with artifices of this kind. We are therefore inclined to assume that in this case, too, a large part of the horizontal thrust is absorbed by the joints through frictional resistance. The fact that the dancing pavilion was combined in every direction with the surrounding halls by a network of architraves, although there was no ritual necessity for this, strengthens our hypothesis that this was intended to divert some of the thrust on to other architectural elements.

Low corbelled domes like that at Mount Ābū are repeatedly encountered in the Jain architecture of north-eastern India. The domes are frequently surrounded by spacious pilaster halls, so that the eight columns below the octagonal architrave should not have to bear the thrust alone. There is no doubt that centring was required in the construction of the vaulting as well as for the pyramid-shaped cross-vaulting of Hindu temples. This costly method – which can be reconstructed with assurance from extant buildings – is only mentioned once in the many manuals on architecture that have survived. In the 'Shilpa-prakāsha' we read the following: 'It is essential to erect in the interior a massive wooden frame. Supported by this, the stone slabs of the roof can be placed in the correct position, one above the other.'

The 'Shilpa-prakāsha' refers in particular to the temple at Caurasi. But it is precisely here that the roof of the mukhashālā could theoretically have been erected without any resort to a temporary framework, for the stone slabs jutting out into the chamber also project on the other side of the wall, partly as extensions of the roof, to such an extent that the resultant of the total weight is still within the limits of the masonry. The gap that remains between the 'arms' was bridged by thin, light stone slabs. Because of this slight extra weight the resultant must have been shifted close to the pivot. Some of the slabs of the roof slope inwards (see plan, p. 171), and only extensive supports in the interior will prevent the roof from collapsing. The slabs would have already fallen if the sthapatis had not devised an ingenious way of arranging them which makes it more difficult for a slab that has already tipped over to slip down. The roof, like the ground-plan, is rectangular in every horizontal section. But the vertical joints in the corbelling were not set at right angles to the ceiling of the chamber; instead they were set radially, as though this were a circular building. If a stone slab tips over, it cannot fall, since it is cut in a conical shape and is held in position by the neighbouring slabs. Another factor making for stability is the irregular and intricate structure of cogged stones. The artifice of cutting the roof slabs radially is also employed at Konārak as well as at Caurasi.

From the reports of those engaged in the restoration work it emerges that four massive stone pillars support the roof of the mandapa at Konārak. The same solution was chosen in the nearby Purī temple as well as in the Kandāriya Mahādeo temple at Khajurāho. In all three cases it was found that the horizontal thrust might force the building to break apart. For this reason the colonnade was made to carry some of the load of the roof. The corbel-vaulting which was added transferred the horizontal thrust to the stout enclosure walls. The lines of force remind us of the system used in Gothic cathedrals, where the vertical loads are carried by a line of pillars and the horizontal thrust is diverted to the buttresses added externally.

Rock-cut architecture

In medieval manuals of architecture there are few detailed references to the mode of construction of a 'structive' temple, since the building of a sanctuary was regarded primarily as a rite. No written information has survived about the way in which a chaitya-hall or a vihāra was carved out of the rock during the predominantly Buddhist period of architecture, from the third century B.C. to the sixth century A.D. The inscriptions 'in situ' praise the donors and explain their social position, but do not give any clues from which we could deduce how the work was carried on, what tools were used, or how long the operation took. Accordingly, if we now endeavour to elucidate the methods used to carve such a cave, we have to rely

An incomplete subterranean monastery at Ajantā, showing the technique of carving out of rock

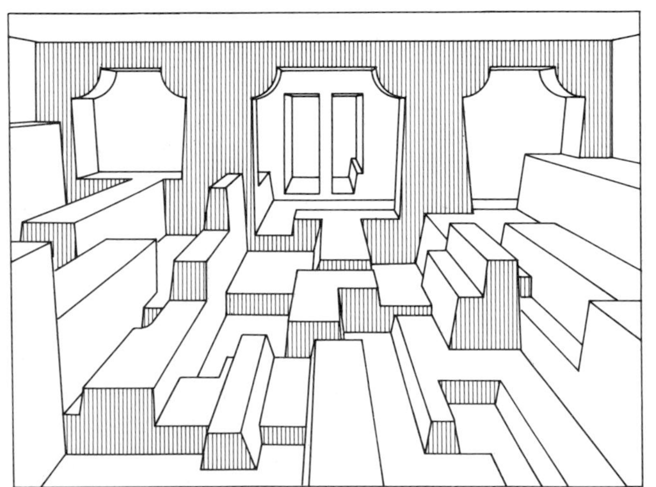

exclusively on observations made in those caves which were not completed. The nature of the tools that were used can also be inferred only from the traces they left behind in the rock. As a rule the main tools were a pointed chisel and an iron mallet. To polish the rock face flat chisels of varying width were employed. Only if the rock was very soft was it possible to start the work with a pick-axe.

First of all the rock face was polished and the façade sketched in and incised. If a high chamber was to be hewn out, the workmen commenced by driving a tunnel as tall as a man into the rock beneath the place where the ceiling would be. This was first widened and then deepened by cutting steps. On each level the stone-mason who did the rough work was followed by another artisan who scarified and polished the walls. In one incomplete cave at Ajantā all the wall faces worked by the pointed chisel also received their final polish. We may assume that here the rough work with the pick-axe and pointed chisel was carried out by the same artisan who, after he had cut away a certain amount of rock, took up his flat chisel and mallet in order to do the detailed work on the wall he had made. While he was working his way deeper into the mountain, using alternately his pick-axe and flat chisel, plasterers and painters followed along behind to begin their work in the front part of the chamber. This theory is corroborated by a rock-cut monastery at Ajantā which shows all three stages in the process.

Besides this method of enlarging an initial working platform, a second method was occasionally employed. The stone-masons dug trenches some 1 to 1.5 metres wide into the ground on the levels where they were working, leaving ribs of rock standing between the trenches, which were roughly the same width. It was then a relatively easy matter to break through these ribs of rock from both sides simultaneously, using several chisels as wedges.

The advantage of the stepped method, by comparison with that of digging shafts, was that the wedges could be driven in vertically, so that the rock which was broken away fell down on to the step immediately

Above: incomplete Hindu rock-cut temple at Mahaballipuram
Below: after completion (reconstruction)

below, and could then easily be carried over the lower steps to the exit. Chaitya-halls were apparently always hewn out in this way. In the first stage of the work the stone-masons penetrated from a tunnel in the crown of the vault downwards to the top of what was to be the colonnade. The rubble could be removed through the horseshoe-shaped sun window. Since the builders were evidently always at pains to avoid introducing wooden scaffolding into the interior, and to execute all the details from a natural rock platform, we may assume that at Kārlī, for example, the wooden ribs were inserted after the first stage of building was over. Not until the barrel roof had obtained its final appearance did work begin on hewing out the lower zone, in the second stage of the operation. Each of the heavy teak ribs measured in cross-section approximately 80 × 25 cm. They had to be made of several planks and were secured by strong dowels to the polished rock surface of the vault. The weight of each rib was about $3\frac{1}{2}$ tons, and many props were required to insert them after the chamber had been carved to its full height.

When the vaulting had been completed, the nave was hewn out of the rock by making steps. The loose rubble from this operation was no longer taken out through the sun window but down the steps and through the door of the nave, which had already been cut through. Finally deep niches were carved in the walls of the nave, and these were joined together to form aisles. The last stage was the working of the columns, which were initially still in a rough state.

Some early Pallava caves at Mahaballipuram provide information about the technique used to hollow out low chambers. The artisans incised the colonnade on the polished rock of the façade and divided up the remaining areas which had to be worked into square panels. Deep grooves were then cut along the incised lines with a pointed chisel, so that regular bosses were left. These protuberances could then easily be hewn off by striking them from the side. When the first layer had been removed, another network of squaring lines was drawn and another ten centimetres of hard granite chiselled away. This process was repeated in the interior of the cave until the chamber reached the desired size. In this case, unlike the Buddhist caves which had been carved earlier, the rough work was done separately from the sculpturing of the detail. Only when the entire rock-cut temple had been given a roughly-hewn surface did the artisans set to work to cut away the final layer of the protuberances, to polish the walls and to finish the columns.

One of the two identical caves in the Barābar Hills, Lomas Rishi, also contains evidence that it was worked in two different stages. One part of the interior was already polished in the way typical of the Mauryan dynasty while other parts of the ceiling and the circular ancillary chamber had not yet been chis-

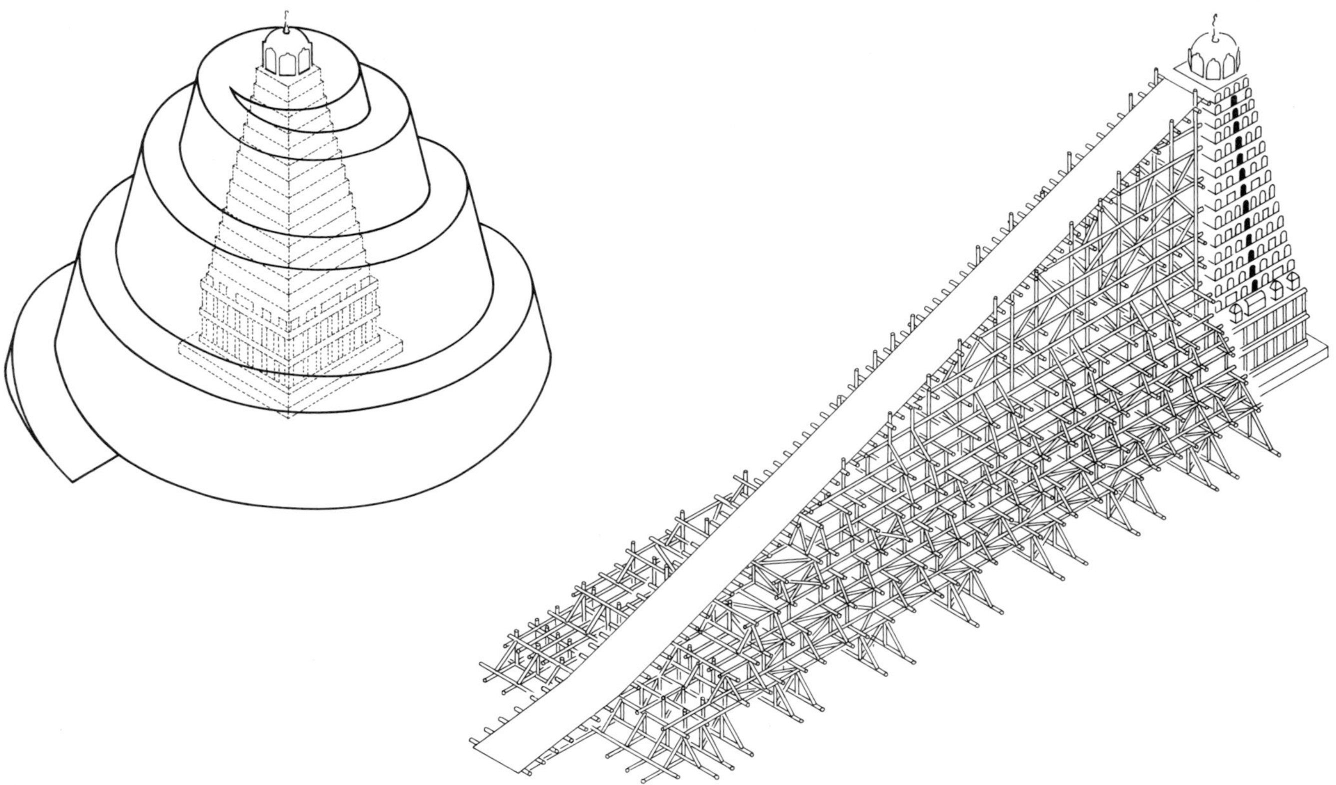

Transport of an 80-ton cap-stone to the top of the temple tower at Tanjore:
a) by a spiral earthen ramp (according to K. Fischer)
b) by a wooden ramp (according to local legend)

elled out even in their rough state. Since the chamber was not excavated from the top downwards but in the reverse direction, when the ceiling was as tall as a man the artisans were faced with the difficult task of chiselling it away from below – out of hard granite. Under these unfavourable conditions the Sudāma cave was the only one of the two which was completed. In this context it is astonishing that, some dozens of years later, it was the incomplete cave, not the glittering Sudāma cave, which was given a magnificent entrance.

Methods of transporting stone

Each of Ashoka's columns, of which about 30 are known to exist, measured some 15 metres in length and weighed 50 tons. Several of these monoliths, erected hundreds of miles apart, originate from the quarry at Chūnar which supplied the material for the honorary umbrella of the stūpa at Sāñchī. At Sāñchī, too, about 500 miles from the quarry, one of these sandstone columns was put up. Transportation by land was certainly out of the question, since this would have meant traversing ravines and impassable jungle. Only one method was left: to build a gigantic raft and to float the stone up the Ganges, the Jumnā and finally the Betwā river, which flows within 2 kilometres of Sāñchī. Since the Betwā hardly carries any water in summer, the column had to be transported during the rainy season. But this was far from an easy matter, since at this time of the year the rivers tend to rise suddenly without warning, and the speed of the current scarcely allows one to drag a big raft upstream. We cannot explain how the column was transported over the remaining 2 kilometres, particularly as a difference of height of 60 metres had to be overcome in the last 200 metres. Nor do we know with what kind of devices the column was erected.

The architects of the Brihadeshvara temple at Tanjore in the eleventh century faced similar problems of transportation. The stout circuit walls of the temple, like the vimāna itself, consist of granite blocks. But there is no granite quarry in close proximity to Tanjore. It is particularly puzzling how the builders managed to place a monolith weighing 80 tons, the main slab covering the crown of the vimāna, in its position 70 metres above ground. There is a small village some 6 kilometres north-west of Tanjore bearing the name Sarapallam ('dell of the scaffold'). According to local legend the stone was taken from this place to its destination at Tanjore up a wooden inclined ramp. But there are a lot of legends about this temple: for example, that the tower does not cast any shadow. And neither of these two stories can be credited.

More realistic than this tale of the wooden ramp is the attempted reconstruction by K. Fischer. He thinks that the temple was surrounded by an earthen rampart and that the top was reached by a spiral road. By this means, with the aid of several elephants, it could have been possible to drag the monolith up the incline on wooden frames.

During the Middle Ages ox-drawn carts were used to transport heavy columns, as may be seen from a drawing on the citadel of Raichur. It is surprising that at this time carts could be made which did not collapse under the weight of such columns (the one depicted weighs some 45 tons).

A passage in the Jain chronicles also contains a reference to the transportation of stones in an ox-drawn cart. The minister Vastupala told his brother Tejapāla about his plan to dedicate a temple at Ābū, similar to the Vimala temple. Tejapāla was enthusiastic about this idea and at once started out for Arasana in order to supervise the quarrying of white marble – twice as much as would probably be needed for the new sanctuary. Like many sacred places in India, Ābū is situated in a high-lying inaccessible valley. Its pleasing landscape of palm-trees is hemmed in by mountains with sheer cliffs dropping to the valley floor. To transport the blocks of marble Tejapāla had a road with a low gradient specially built, which extended from the plain to the highest point in the Ābū valley. Only slowly and in stages were the vehicles able to make their way uphill. Tejapāla's brother-in-law, Udala, was put in charge of the building operations. Along the road he had resting places built where men and animals were taken care of. After all the marble had been transported to the building site, the road was destroyed to prevent the Muslim raiders who roamed the country from penetrating into this secluded and sacred high-lying valley.

In reconstructing ancient Indian methods of transportation we must take into account the fact that

Transport of a stone pillar by ox-cart. After a relief from the citadel of Raichur

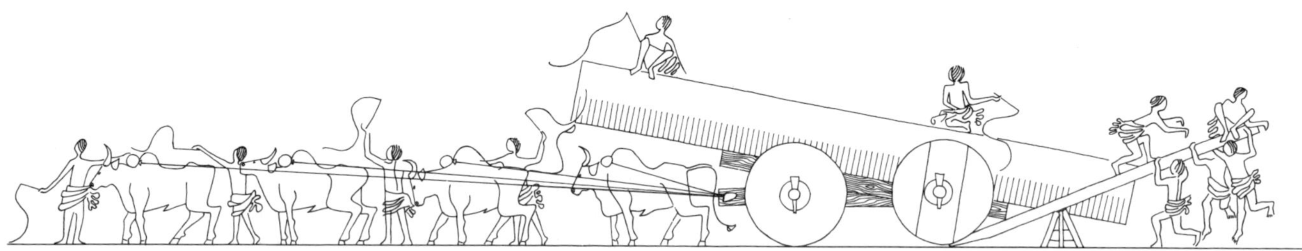

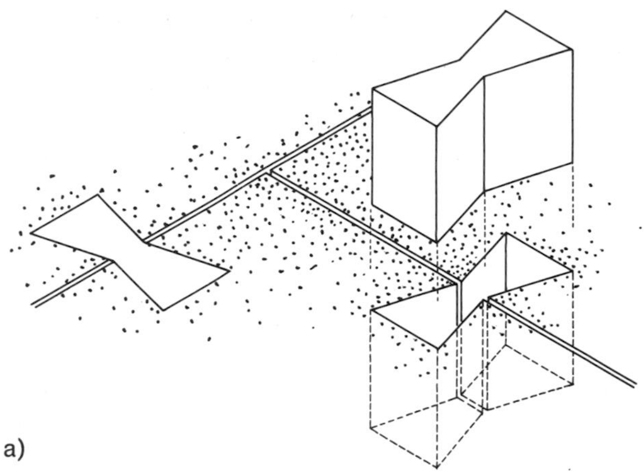

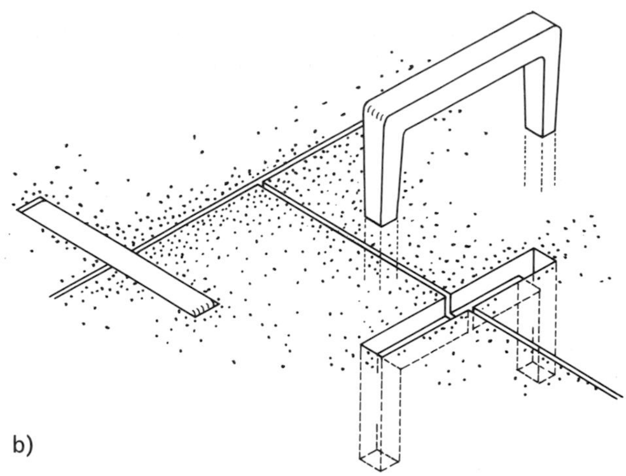

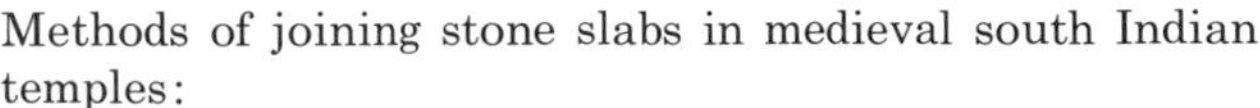

Methods of joining stone slabs in medieval south Indian temples:
a) with a moulded stone
b) with an iron cramp

elephants were available to help move heavy loads. It is true that elephants are unsuitable as draught animals, but they can push heavy loads along with their trunks. Local people say that particularly large slabs were occasionally placed in position on the building site itself with the aid of wedges and levers. By putting several elephants on the longer arm of the lever, even the heaviest loads could be raised. The movement of building materials, especially of slabs, up to the top courses of a north Indian shikhara was effected with the aid of wooden scaffolding if the height involved was not too great. In the legends spun about every large sanctuary we are often told that high towers were surrounded by a mound of earth. It is tempting to conclude from this that in all parts of India, and not only at Tanjore, it was common practice to transport stone slabs by means of earth ramps, either spiral or straight, such as are known from ancient Egypt. From Konārak we are told that the interior of the mukhashālā was filled with dry sand from the surrounding dunes up to the level where work was in progress, in order to prevent the corbelled ceiling from collapsing during the operation. After the roof was completed, the sand was removed through the three outer doors of the building.

South Indian gopuras have stone only in the lower storey; all the upper storeys are of brick. In the interior of the tower the storage rooms become progressively narrower towards the top, corresponding to the tiered division of the façade. All the bricks, wooden beams, supports and the plaster etc. used for stucco work had to be transported up to a considerable height. The light bamboo scaffolding which was put up around the tower while the exterior was being plastered and painted was not suited for the hoisting of such loads. The architects therefore devised a means of raising them which could be used not only during the progress of the building work but afterwards as well. They left square holes free in the centre of each storey in the tower, one over the other, and through them building materials could easily be hoisted up to any height.

Stone working

The earliest monumental structures in India were rock-cut caves. The chief reason why 'structive' temples in quarried stone were built, from the seventh century onward, was probably that there was no monolith of adequate size available at some site which, according to the astrologers, was suited for the manifestation of one of the deities.

The temple was regarded by the Indian sthapati not as a monument but as a plastic material dimension of the god. It was hardly of any interest to him, so far as we can tell from the ancient manuscripts, that the temple was of necessity composed of walls, ceilings and supports. The favoured monolithic way of building was kept to even after temples had already been built in ashlar masonry for several centuries. The walls of the temple and the sanctuary were usually built up of rectangular, pointed, scarified and polished squared ashlar. From this rough form, as though from a monolith, the stone-masons chiselled the curved outline of a north Indian shikhara or south Indian pilastered structures such as that at Tanjore. This method can be studied particularly well at Tanjore, where the joints between the stone slabs are only occasionally and haphazardly in harmony with the architectonic form: they run slantwise across overhanging cornices or cut through a row of pilasters in an arbitrary way. The advantage of working stone in its final position was that one did not have to be too accurate in setting the blocks, which were often very large, since they were not yet in their final form. Designing was also simplified, since the size and shape of each slab did not have to be determined in advance. The disadvantage was that one had to transport far larger quantities of stone than if each slab were worked first and then set.

We note with surprise that also in the corbel vaults of north Indian mukhashālās the formally accentuated corbelling occasionally does not tally with the actual stratification of the stone. At Bhuvaneshvar we find several examples of corbel vaults where the stones are not even set in courses at all. Squared ashlar blocks of varying size were assembled to produce the rough form of a corbel vault and then the geometric form of a vault was elaborated from this 'constructed monolith'. This method, too, naturally had its disadvantages. For example, it could happen that a small stone was worked on to such an extent that it dropped out of the ceiling or wall. For this reason as time went on the crude form was increasingly approximated to the final one. In the Rājarāni temple at Bhuvaneshvar or the Sūrya temple at Konārak – in both cases crude unworked parts have survived – the difference was reduced to a minimum; only the profiles and the figured decoration still had to be hewn out once the stones were in place.

The same monolithic method of working was applied to roughly-hewn blocks of marble by the Jain builders at Mount Ābū. The fine filigree work on the columns and mouldings, fabulous tracery in marble, could be produced only with a file instead of a chisel. The temple chronicles relate that the artisans, most of whom were ivory-carvers, were paid according to the weight of powdered stone which they filed off each day.

Vimala Sah is said to have paid 185.3 million rupees for the construction of the Vimala temple. The building site which he had to purchase from the Brahmins measures some 43 × 28 metres. He covered this area with the gold coins then in currency, each of which covered approximately 6.5 square centimetres and cost about 25 rupees. The price came to about 38,450 rupees per square metre. Thus for a total area of 1204 square metres Vimala Sah must have paid 46 million rupees, leaving a sum of 139 million rupees for the actual building – which seems credible.

The Pallavas endeavoured to give additional stability to the carefully worked joins between the stones, which were set without mortar, by inserting into the masonry at regular intervals thin layers of large granite panels. Such 'binders' were of particular importance when a wall or ceiling was constructed in two shells and the intervening space was filled in with rubble. At Orissā, at the beginning of the second millennium, artisans began joining the stones of each course directly to one another. On both sides of the join dovetailed depressions were chiselled out and a moulded stone fitted in. This involved a particularly great expenditure of effort. After a course of rough stones had been set, several hundred holes had to be hollowed out accurately to receive the corresponding cramps used to hold the masonry together. These cramps were only laid horizontally; vertical joins were unusual.

At Konārak we can see joins like those familiar from Greek temples. At a distance of some six centimetres from the joint, holes were drilled into the stones; a groove was cut between them and an iron cramp driven into the depression. At Konārak iron was used both to hold together different courses of stone and also to reinforce various stone structures. The discovery that a corbel vault loses its equilibrium as soon as c > w led to the device of erecting four massive pillars in the interior of the mukhashālā at Konārak. These were designed to divert some of the weight of the roof above the square of architraves. However, the structure as a whole, with its enormous dimensions, did not seem sufficiently safe to the architects, who tried to fortify the masonry of the pyramid-shaped roof, and all the architraves provided for in the building, by placing wrought iron rods into the masonry and also below the architraves. Most of these iron props are between 10 and 15 centimetres in diameter, but at particularly dangerous points regular iron under-props 25 centimetres high were used. In view of the otherwise relatively simple building techniques employed, we note with astonishment that the builders had a clear appreciation of the advantages of iron and knew how to apply it to good effect. Stone architraves with iron under-props play a role, from the point of view of statics, comparable to the steel bars in reinforced concrete. The compressive stresses which make themselves felt in the upper part of a support can be carried by the stone architrave; on the other hand, the tensile stresses which occur in the lower zone cannot be carried by stone, but can easily be carried by iron. In reinforced concrete work it is a prerequisite, if such a construction is to be efficient, that the steel and the concrete should be firmly joined to each other. At Konārak, it is true, the stone and the iron rods do not form such an effective unit from the point of view of statics. Nevertheless the heavy loads upon the supports of the 'reinforced' architraves to some extent have the effect of binding the stone and iron, either by extreme compression or by a high degree of frictional resistance.

Chronological Table

B. C.	**History of India**
2500–1500	Height of Indus civilization
1500	Aryan invasion
800	The 'Vedas' put into writing
563–483	Gautama Buddha, 'the Enlightened One'
326–325	Alexander's Indian campaign
273–232	Emperor Ashoka of the Maurya dynasty
	Spread of Buddhism throughout Maurya empire
185–72	Shunga dynasty in north India
20	First envoy from south India to Augustus Caesar

B. C.	**Monuments**
	Early cities, Mohenjo-daro and Harappā
	First corbel arches
250	Edict pillars of Ashoka
	Lomas Rishi cave
	Sudāma cave
	Brick stūpa at Sāñchī
150	Extension of stūpa at Sāñchī
	First Hīnayāna halls at Ajantā
1st cent.	Chaitya-halls at Kārlī
25	Toranas at Sāñchī

A. D.	**History of India**
120–162	Kanishka of the Kushan dynasty
320–499	Gupta dynasty
465	Invasion of White Huns under Toramāna
543–757	Early Chalukya dynasty in south India
757–900	South India under Pallava rule
760–800	Krishna I, Rāshtrakūta dynasty, in central India
846–1279	Chola dynasty in south India
973–1189	Late Chalukya dynasty
986	Sabuktigin of Ghaznī invades India
997–1030	Mahmud of Ghaznī makes 17 raids into India
1111–1310	Hoysala dynasty
1206	Qutb-ud-din Aibak, first Sultan of Delhi
1371	Islamic state of Madurai, founded by Mohamud bin Tuglakh, conquered by Hindu kings of Vijayanagar
1526–1857	Moghul dynasties in north and central India
1529–1736	Last flowering of Hindu kingdoms in south India
1772–1785	Warren Hastings, first British Governor-General

A. D.	**Monuments**
2nd cent.	Last Hīnayāna halls at Ajantā
	Stūpa court at Takht-i-Bāhi
450	Lādh Khān temple at Aihole
500	Durgā temple at Aihole
450–642	Mahāyāna halls at Ajantā
650	Shore temples at Mahaballipuram
650	Rathas at Mahaballipuram
700	Shore temples at Mahaballipuram
8th cent.	Kailāsa temple at Elūrā
	First mention of Madurai
975	Mukteshvara temple at Bhuvaneshvar
1010	Brihadeshvara temple at Tanjore
950–1050	Temple at Khajurāho
1021	Vimala temple at Mount Ābū
1075	Brahmeshvara temple at Bhuvaneshvar
1200	Rājarāni temple at Bhuvaneshvar
1230	Tejapāla temple at Mount Ābū
1250	Sūrya temple at Konārak
1268	Keshava temple at Somnāthpur
13th to 17th cent.	Expansion of temple city of Madurai
	Enlargement of many temple cities in south India

es and diagrams are as follows
right; l = left):

of India: 17/18, 41 la, 41 r, 48, 56,
, 99, 100 r, 104, 106, 133 b, 134, 138 l,

7, 100 l, 136, 145, 148

a, 42 r

80 l

96

591

9

.: 45

).: 44

n, A.: 42 lb, 51, 52, 53, 54, 55 r, 57, 87, 88 r, 94, 102,
, 138 r, 141, 142, 149, 151, 152, 171, 176, 178, 179,
2

uotation on page 12 is from S. Radhakrishnan and
les A. Moore (ed.), *Indian Philosophy*. Princeton Press,
bay, 1957, pp. 274–275.

Glossary

Ājīvikas	monks of a sect which evolved from Jainism
āmalaka (m.)	crowning member of a temple, in the chape of a flat seed-capsule
anda (n.)	literally, egg; the hemispherical dome of a stūpa
apsaras (f.)	celestial nymphs
Aryans	tribes of herdsmen and horsemen who migrated into India during the 2nd millennium B.C.
bada (m.)	base of a shikhara
beki (m.)	literally, neck; slab between chapra and āmalaka
bhakti-yoga (m.)	way of love and devotion; worship as ritual
bhoga-mandir (n.)	sacrificial pavilion
Bodhisattva (m.)	Buddhist saint; 'not-yet-Buddha'
Brahmā (m.)	Lord, God the Creator
Brahman (m., n.)	world soul, supreme principle of order
Brahman, Brahmin (n.)	member of priest and ruling caste
Brahmā-sthāna (m.)	panel in centre of a mandala
chaitya (m.)	shrine, altar
chaitya-hall	Buddhist prayer-hall, basilica
Chandellas	north Indian dynasty, 9th–12th cent. A.D.
chapra (f.)	tower with parabolic outline
chatushālā	house built around a court
Cholas	south Indian dynasty, 9th–13th cent. A.D.
deva (m.)	literally, 'the lustrous one'
devadāsī (f.)	temple dancing-girl
dravida style	architectural style in south India
Dravidians	dark-skinned indigenous population of India
dvishālā (f.)	angular building
ekshālā (f.)	simple, not squared off, element of building
Gandhāra	region and kingdom in north of West Pakistan
garbha-griha	literally, womb: cella of a Hindu temple
gopura (n.)	tower surmounting gate
gudha-mandapa (n.)	porch of temple, in north-west India
Gujarat	region in north-west India
Guptas	dynasty, 4th–6th cent. A.D.
harmikā (f.)	shrine, stylized railing round the chattrāvalī
Hīnayāna (n.)	literally, small vehicle: early monastic Buddhism, originally atheistic
Indra (m.)	supreme Vedic deity; god of thunder and lightning
Ishvara (m.)	God, Lord of the World
jagamohan (n.)	assembly hall
Jains	members of a sect founded by Mahāvīra, a contemporary of the Buddhā
jātakas	tales of previous incarnations of the Buddha
jñāna-yoga (m.)	the way of knowledge
Kailāsa (m.)	sacred peak in Himalayas, the seat of Shiva
kalasha	finial of tower, in the shape of a vase, on temples in north India
karma yoga (m.)	the way of unselfish action
Keshava (m.)	aspect of Vishnu
konaka-ratha (m.)	(or konaga-paga): projecting corner pillar of a shikhara
Kshatriya (m.)	member of warrior caste
kudū	horseshoe-shaped window in façade of a chaitya-hall
lingam (n.)	phallus, symbolic of Shiva
Magadha	kingdom in north India
mahā-mandapa (n.)	literally, large hall
Mahāyāna	literally, 'great vehicle': theistic form of Buddhism
mahā yuga	'great age' in cosmology (4,320,000 years)
mithuna	pairs of lovers
Mānasāra (n.)	medieval manual of architecture
mandala (n.)	magic sign
mandūka- (n.)	ground-plan divided into 64 (8 × 8) squares
padma-garbha- (n.)	ground-plan divided into 256 (16 × 16) squares
parama-shayika- (n.)	ground-plan divided into 81 (9 × 9) squares
sthandila- (n.)	ground-plan divided into 49 (7 × 7) squares
vāstu-purusha- (n.)	magic sign which overcomes the demon residing in the building
mandapa (n.)	assembly porch of a temple, in south India
mantram (n.)	prayer formula
marma (n.)	intersection point of two lines separating pādas
Mauryas	dynasty, 4th–2nd cent. B.C.

medhi (f.)	base of a stūpa
mudrā	symbolic and ritual gestures
mukhashālā (f.)	assembly porch of a temple, in north India
nāgara style	literally, city-dwellers' style: architectural style in north India
Nandi (m.)	bull, Shiva's mount
nandi-mandapa (n.)	pavilion containing image of Nandi
nat-mandir (n.)	dance pavilion in temples at Orissā
nav-choki (n.)	portico between gudha-mandapa and nat-mandir
nirvāna	void, extinction
pāda (m.)	square area forming part of a mandala
paga (m.)	synonym of ratha; pilaster-like projection
Panjab	literally, land of the five rivers: region in north India and West Pakistan
pida (m.)	terraced roof terminating the mukhashālā
pida-deul	building with a mukhashālā
pradakshinā (f.)	rite of circumambulation of a cult object
pradakshinā-patha (m.)	path along which pradakshinā procession moves
pūjā (n.)	Hindu religious service with sacrifice
Purusha (m.)	primeval human being or spirit, personification of the cosmos
rāja (m.)	king
rāja-yoga (m.)	the royal way of becoming one with the Brahmā
ranga-mandapa (n.)	literally, polychrome hall: dance pavilion in Jain temple
ratha (m.)	a) temple conceived as a chariot b) pilaster-like projection or recess in façade of temple in nāgara style
rekhā-deul	cella with square ground-plan, in north India
Shakas	dynasty, 1st–4th cent. A.D.
shakti (f.)	female aspect of a god
shikhara (m.)	tower of a temple, in north India
Shilpa-prakāsha (n.)	medieval manual of architecture
Shiva (m.)	God the Destroyer
Shivaites	Hindus who regard Shiva as the supreme god
Shūdra (m.)	member of agricultural labouring class
Shungas	dynasty, 2nd–1st cent. B.C.
Solankīs	Chalukya dynasty from Gujarat
stambha (m.)	column, often free-standing
sthapati (m.)	priest-architect
stūpa (m.)	hemispherical burial or reliquary mound
Sūrya (m.)	sun god
swastika (m.)	swastika, hooked cross
tantra (n.)	esoteric doctrine
thabha (m.)	post of a railing
torana (m.)	gateway
triratna	literally, three jewels: Buddhist symbol
trishālā (f.)	house built around court open on one side
Upanishads	philosophical additions to the Vedas
Vaishya (m.)	member of the trading caste
vajralepa (m.)	transparent paste used for stones
Vajrayāna (n.)	literally, diamond vehicle: Tantric form of Buddhism
Vārāhī (f.)	goddess, 'one of the seven mothers'
vāstu (n.)	a) building site b) remainder (after a division)
vāstu-purusha (m.)	demon who resides at every building site
vāstu-vidyā (f.)	doctrine of architecture, architectural theory
Veda (m.)	collection of scripture containing primeval revelations
vedikā (f.)	railing
vesara style	architectural style, a blend of north and south Indian elements
vihāra (m.)	Buddhist monastery
vimāna (m.)	tower of temple, in south India; chart of the heavens
Vishnu (m.)	God the Preserver
yantram (n.)	magic symbol, diagram or instrument
Yavana (m.)	Greek
yoga (m.)	literally, way: the way of becoming one with Brahman
yogini-yantram (n.)	yantram from Orissā, made up of triangles
yuga (n.)	age of the world, in cosmology

Bibliography

Acharya, P.K.
An Encyclopaedia of Hindu Architecture. London, O.U.P., 1927–1946

Annual Reports of the Archaeological Survey of India, Calcutta – New Delhi

Bhattacharya, T.
The Canons of Indian Art. Calcutta, Mukhopadyay, 1963

Boner, A. and Rath Sharmā, S.
Shilpa-prakāsha. Leyden, Brill, 1966

Brown, P.
Indian Architecture. Bombay, Taraporevala, 1965

Coomaraswamy, A.K.
History of Indian and Indonesian Art. New York, Dover Publications, 1965

Diez, E.
Die Kunst Indiens. Berlin, Athenaion, 1925

Fabri, Ch.
An Introduction to Indian Architecture. Bombay, Asia Publishing House, 1963

Fergusson, J.
History of Indian and Eastern Architecture. Delhi, Munshiram Manoharlal, 1967

Fischer, K.
Schöpfungen indischer Kunst. Cologne, DuMont Schauberg, 1959

Frédéric, L.
L'Inde: ses temples, ses sculptures. Paris, Arts et Métiers Graphiques, 1959

Gangoly, O.C.
Indian Architecture. Bombay, Kutub Publishers, 1954

Goetz, H.
India: Five Thousand Years of Indian Art. London, Methuen, 1960; 2nd imprint, 1964

K…
Th…

La R…
Indisc…

Marshall, …
The Monu…
Archaeolog…

Rambach, P. a…
L'Inde – Images…

Rowland, B.
The Art and Archite…
of Art.) Harmondswo…

Shukla, D.N.
Vāstu-Shāstra, vol. I. Bha…
Chandigarh, Punjab Unive…

Wu, Nelson
Chinese and Indian Architectu…
G. Braziller, 1963

Zimmer, H.
The Art of Indian Asia. Bollinger se…

Acknowledgements

The references in the figu…
(a = above; b = below; r …

Acharya, P.K.: 49
Archaeological Survey…
59/60, 88 l, 95, 98 a, 98 b…
146, 172, 181
Batley, C.: 41 lb
Brown, P.: 13, 91, 9…
Fergusson, J.: 42…
Fischer, K.: 90, …
Gangoly, O.C.: …
Kramrisch, S. …
Rowland, B. …
Shukla, D.N…
Sompura, …
Volwahse…
105, 133…
180 r, 18…

The …
Cha…
Bo…

List of plates

List of plans